HMS
BELFAST

HMS
BELFAST

CRUISER 1939

Richard Johnstone-Bryden

Seaforth
PUBLISHING

Copyright © Richard Johnstone-Bryden

First published in Great Britain in 2013 by
Seaforth Publishing,
Pen & Sword Books Ltd,
47 Church Street,
Barnsley S70 2AS

www.seaforthpublishing.com

British Library Cataloguing in Publication Data

A catalogue record for this book is available from the
British Library

ISBN 978 1 84832 155 7

Design by Stephen Dent
Deck layouts by Tony Garrett
Printed and bound in China

CONTENTS

Half title: Normally, the Union Flag can only be used as a jack by HM ships. However, in a bid to maintain as much of the cruiser's naval character as possible, the HMS *Belfast* Trust was given permission in 1971 for *Belfast* to wear the White Ensign and a Union Flag as a jack. The signal flags on the foremast's port side middle signal halyard indicate the ship's international call sign GGCN, while those on the inner signal halyard represent the cruiser's pennant number C35 which was painted on the stern and both sides of the hull following her 1956–59 modernisation.

Title pages: *Belfast* is still dressed overall for major occasions. In this case, she is seen shortly before the wedding of Their Royal Highnesses The Duke and Duchess of Cambridge in April 2011. Historically, the junior captain of a fleet or squadron drew up the order of flags to be worn. In 1889 the Admiralty introduced strict instructions to regulate the dressing of ships.

Above left: *Belfast*'s 4in guns, raked funnels and Admiralty Disruptive Camouflage Type 25 provide a contrast to the modern glass facades of the office blocks that now form her backdrop. *(Julian Mannering)*

1 | DESIGN AND CONSTRUCTION

OVER FORTY YEARS AGO, HMS *BELFAST* WAS saved from the scrapman's blowtorch to act as a lasting reminder of the powerful big-gun armoured warships that formed the backbone of the Royal Navy in the first half of the twentieth century. Her smart appearance earned *Belfast* the nickname 'Tiddley B', while her action-packed naval career included the capture of the German liner *Cap Norte*, the battle of North Cape, the D-Day landings, the Yangtze Incident, and the Korean War.

With a standard displacement of 11,550 tons, a main armament of twelve 6in guns and a top speed of 32 knots, the 613ft *Belfast*, together with her ill-fated sister ship *Edinburgh*, were among the largest cruisers ever built for the Royal Navy. The term 'cruiser', originally spelt cruizer, dates back to the eighteenth century, when the word 'cruizing' was used to describe warships undertaking independent operations away from the fleet. Typical missions included hunting for privateers and enemy shipping, or gathering intelligence. Such duties were usually assigned to large frigates, although sloops and brigs also performed this task. Thus in its earliest use, the word cruiser defined a warship's role, rather than a specific type of ship.

The advent of steam propulsion and iron armour in the mid nineteenth century led to a shift in the definition towards describing a specific type of medium-sized long-range warship capable of undertaking the traditional cruising role. Three types of cruiser were built for the Royal Navy between the late nineteenth century and World War I. Armoured cruisers were equipped with the strongest protection, in the form of side and deck armour which inevitably hindered their maximum speed. Protected cruisers achieved higher speeds at the expense of a reduction in the thickness of the side armour, while light cruisers were smaller, faster, and fitted with the least amount of protection. However, during WWI the size and main armament of the light cruiser steadily increased.

The development of cruisers during the interwar years was governed by international treaties in a bid to prevent another costly arms race between the naval powers. The 1921 Washington Treaty restricted cruisers to a maximum gun calibre of 8in and a standard displacement of 10,000 tons. These limits spawned the so-called 'treaty cruisers' that were built up to these allowances. However, the Royal Navy changed tack in the late 1920s, due to the prospect of diminishing funds and the imposition of tonnage quotas by future arms limitation treaties. Rather than build cruisers of

Belfast is seen alongside her fitting out berth in the Harland & Wolff shipyard shortly after her launch in 1938. (*Maritime Photo Library*)

Still wearing the Red Ensign, *Belfast* undertakes her final acceptance trials. On completion of these trials the cruiser anchored in Belfast Lough where Captain G A Scott, DSO, RN, accepted her from the builders on behalf of the Admiralty and the chaplain conducted the commissioning service on 5 August 1939. (*Maritime Photo Library*)

the maximum permitted size, the Admiralty decided to lay down a larger number of cheaper, smaller cruisers to fulfil its extensive colonial and trade protection commitments.

The anticipated tonnage quotas were introduced by the 1930 London Treaty, which split each country's permitted allowance up to 31 December 1936 between Type A (heavy cruisers), defined as being armed with a gun calibre in excess of 6.1in, and Type B (light cruisers), with guns of less than 6.1in calibre.

However, the Admiralty was forced to reconsider its approach when it received reports that Japan had laid down two 8,500-ton cruisers armed with fifteen 6.1in guns, mounted in five triple turrets. It subsequently emerged that the *Mogami* class actually displaced 12,400 tons and the 6.1in guns could be exchanged for 8in guns. The Americans responded to the Japanese cruisers by laying down the 10,000-ton *Brooklyn* class, which also sported a main armament of fifteen 6in guns, mounted in five triple turrets, and could reach a top speed of 32 knots.

These designs reflected the view that a higher number of 6in guns could achieve a rapid rate of fire which outweighed the benefits of the greater range and heavier shells fired by a smaller number of slower-firing 8in guns. Provided that a heavily armed 6in cruiser possessed a good turn of speed, along with enough protection to withstand hits by 8in shells, it would be capable of successfully engaging an adver-

sary by swiftly closing the range and rapidly engulfing its target with a considerable number of shells.

The Royal Navy embraced this philosophy by developing the 591ft *Southampton*-class cruisers. Armed with twelve 6in guns, mounted in four triple turrets, the 9,100-ton warships were also equipped with eight 4in guns, six 21in torpedoes and two Supermarine Walrus amphibious reconnaissance aircraft. The first pair were included within the 1933 Naval Estimates under their original names of *Minotaur* and *Polyphemus*. The ships were subsequently known as either the *Southampton* or 'Town' class, following the Admiralty's decision to rename the first two ships *Southampton* and *Newcastle*. The remaining trio of Group One ships was authorised a year later while the three slightly enlarged members of Group Two were incorporated in the 1935 and 1936 Estimates.

Before placing orders for the third group of *Southampton*-class cruisers, the Admiralty considered increasing the armament to sixteen 6in guns, mounted in four quadruple turrets, to compete more closely with the firepower of the *Mogami* and *Brooklyn* classes. However, the quadruple mountings proved difficult to develop and were dropped in favour of improved versions of the triple turrets fitted to the earlier *Southampton*s. The weight saved by this decision enabled the thickness of the deck armour to be increased. Other notable changes included a greater displacement of 11,550 tons, lengthening the hull by 22ft, mounting the aft 6in turrets one deck higher, fitting an additional pair of twin 4in turrets amidships, and moving the machinery spaces 20ft aft, which in turn forced the funnels to be relocated by a similar amount to alter the external profile. Whilst *Belfast* and *Edinburgh* formed Group Three of the *Southampton* class, they were often referred to as the *Edinburgh* class.

Having approved the final design for the two ships on 28 May 1936, the Admiralty placed the contract for *Belfast*'s construction with Harland & Wolff in her namesake city on 21 September. The shipyard awarded the cruiser the symbolic ship number 1000 and laid her keel on 10 December 1936. The Prime Minister's wife, Anne Chamberlain, travelled to the city's Queen's Island to launch the cruiser on St Patrick's Day, 17 March 1938. Fourteen months later *Belfast* sailed from Northern Ireland for twelve days of

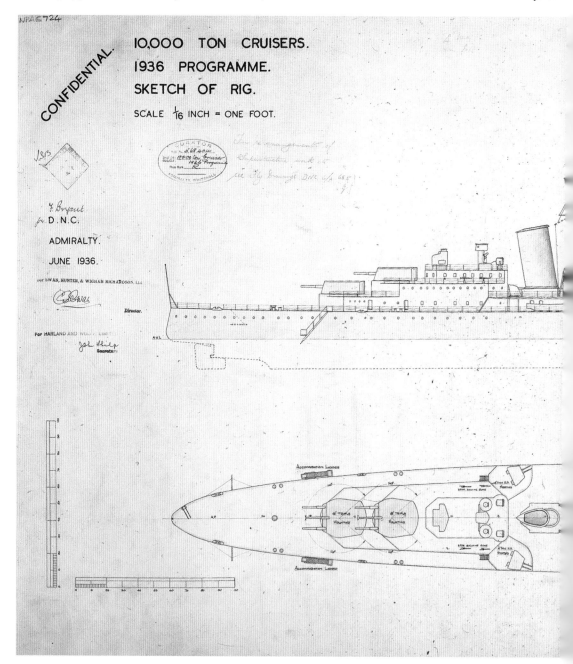

trials and reached a maximum speed of 32.98 knots on the Arran measured mile. She returned to Harland and Wolff for the finishing touches prior to her completion on 3 August 1939. Two days later, whilst at anchor in Belfast Lough, Captain G A Scott, DSO, RN, formally accepted the cruiser on behalf of the Admiralty shortly before the commissioning ceremony. According to the Navy Estimates, she had cost £2,141,514 to build, including £75,000 for the armament.

Dated June 1936, this 1:192 scale plan illustrates the original outboard profile of *Belfast* and her ill-fated sister ship *Edinburgh* including the arrangements for the walrus aircraft, the original forward superstructure, tripod masts, aft pair of 4in guns, the first boat deck and the relatively open layout of 02 Deck. (© *National Maritime Museum, Greenwich, London, NPA6724*)

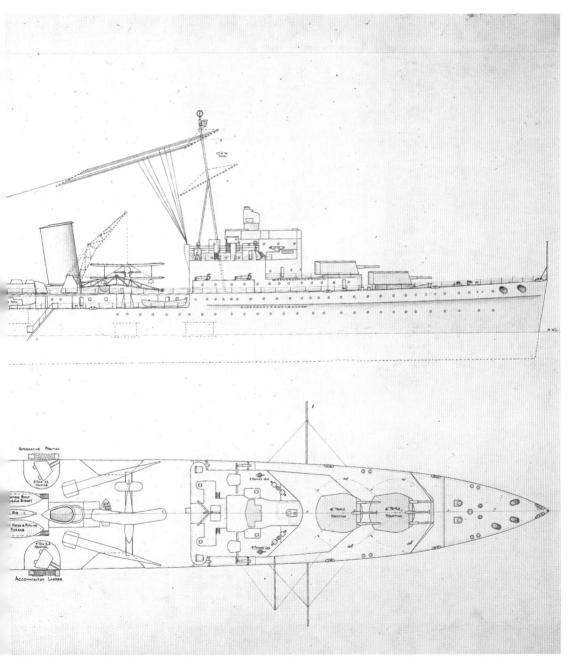

2 | FIRST COMMISSION AUGUST TO NOVEMBER 1939

WITH THE CLOUDS OF WAR RAPIDLY GATHERING across Europe, the Navy's latest cruiser sailed from Northern Ireland to Portsmouth where she joined the Home Fleet's 2nd Cruiser Squadron. The highlight of *Belfast*'s brief pre-war service occurred in mid August when she played the role of the cruiser *Admiral Hipper* in a major Home Fleet exercise to simulate the breakout of a German surface raider into the North Atlantic. *Belfast* eluded her pursuers off Scotland by escaping under the cover of darkness via the Pentland Firth to successfully fulfil her inaugural assignment.

Within a fortnight, the time for rehearsals had passed as the Fleet took up its war stations on 31 August, and *Belfast* joined the 18th Cruiser Squadron at Scapa Flow. Three days later, the ship's company were at Sunday divisions when the Prime Minister, Neville Chamberlain, announced that war had been declared on Germany. The cruiser spent the majority of September operating between the Faroes and Iceland as part of the Northern Patrol, which had been established on 6 September to enforce the British blockade of Germany. In addition to hunting for enemy raiders,

Belfast searched for eastbound merchant ships attempting to deliver supplies to Germany.

Her repeated sweeps of these hostile waters culminated in the seizure of three ships on 9 October, including the 499ft SS *Cap Norte* of the Hamburg Sud-American Line, which was intercepted fifty miles north-west of the Faroes. Wearing a neutral Swedish Ensign, the 13,615-ton German liner had been repainted and given the false identity of SS *Ancona*. However, *Belfast*'s sharp-eyed Officer of the Watch Lieutenant Alan Seale noticed that *Ancona* had been painted over the name *Cap Norte*. In view of this discrepancy, Captain Scott sent across an armed boarding party, led by Lieutenant Seale, to determine the facts. They swiftly confirmed the liner's true identity and discovered a group of German reservists who were being smuggled back home from Argentina. Once they had taken control of *Cap Norte*, the prize crew began the 500-mile voyage to Kirkwall, where the Germans were interned. Although the poor weather had deterred the *Cap Norte*'s captain from issuing orders to scuttle his ship at the time of her interception, the crew still

In this view of *Belfast* taken shortly after her commissioning in August 1939, it is possible to see her port side triple torpedo tubes through the open firing ports while one of the 27ft whalers that were stowed on gantries under the flight deck has been swung out in case it is required. The hull's original profile prior to the fitting of the two bulges is also clearly evident. (*The Medway Studio*)

Belfast's repeated sweeps of the hostile waters between the Faroes and Iceland as part of the Northern Patrol resulted in the successful interception of three blockade runners on 9 October 1939 including the 13,615 ton SS *Cap Norte*. In this recreation of the stand-off between the two ships, the cruiser's guns are trained towards *Cap Norte* as the boarding party, under the command of Lt Alan Seale, approach the German liner in a small cutter to determine the ship's identity and the nature of its contents. *(© Imperial War Museum, Art. IWM ART 16081)*

planned to do so by causing a diversion on arrival in Kirkwall. Fortunately, one of the British engineers, George Finch, heard about their scheme and managed to avert the situation by arranging for armed reinforcements to board the liner when she reached the Orkneys. Thus she became the largest mid-ocean prize to be seized and brought safely to port in World War II. In an ironic twist of fate, *Cap Norte*, by then converted into a British troopship and renamed HMT *Empire Trooper*, was damaged by shellfire when *Admiral Hipper* opened fire on the southbound Middle East troop convoy WS5A on 25 December 1940.

The triumph of *Cap Norte's* capture turned to tragedy six weeks later when a violent explosion rocked *Belfast* as she sailed from the Firth of Forth for a gunnery exercise with *Southampton* and two destroyers on 21 November 1939. At first Captain Scott assumed that the cruiser had been torpedoed, even though none of the ship's lookouts had spotted either a track or discharge burst. The initial damage report revealed that the blast had disabled the engines and caused twenty-one casualties – nineteen of whom had suffered broken bones due to the violent whipping caused by the explosion. Preparations were made to lower the rafts and floats,

while the nearby tug *Krooman* took the stricken cruiser in tow to Rosyth where she entered dry dock on arrival.

In his official report, Captain Scott concluded that *Belfast* had probably struck at least one mine. He reached this verdict based on the frequent alterations in course immediately before the blast and the fact that nothing had been seen by the numerous lookouts to indicate a torpedo attack. The subsequent survey revealed that the explosion had caused extensive shock damage and broken *Belfast's* back between the bridge and the forward funnel. Had the incident occurred in the later stages of the war, she would probably have been scrapped. However, the Royal Navy could not afford to sacrifice such a valuable warship at this point in the conflict and authorised an extended refit to be undertaken by Devonport Dockyard. Temporary repairs were carried out in Rosyth before she left under the cover of darkness on 28 June 1940, bound for Devonport where she arrived on the night of 4 July. Shortly afterwards, *Belfast's* temporary commanding officer, Captain Blackman, DSO, RN, and his skeleton crew were reassigned to other duties to leave a Special Complement of three officers and a dozen ratings who stood by the ship for the bulk of the refit.

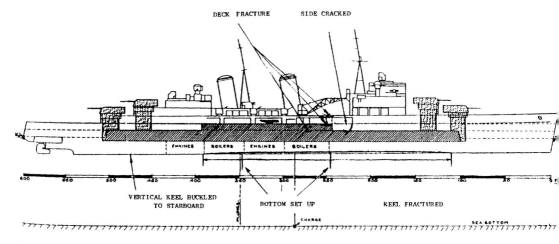

DECK FRACTURE   SIDE CRACKED

ENGINES   BOILERS   ENGINES   BOILERS

VERTICAL KEEL BUCKLED
TO STARBOARD

BOTTOM SET UP   KEEL FRACTURED

CHARGE

SEA BOTTOM

This drawing clearly illustrates the extent of the damage caused by the German magnetic mine in the Firth of Forth on 21 November 1939. The explosion bent the ship up by 4ft 6in and badly dished the starboard side of the hull over a length of 20ft below the forward boiler room. Other damage included the fracturing of the flat keel, a 14in deep buckle in the upper deck, several broken deck plates, and extensive shock damage to the ship's machinery. Had the incident occurred in the latter stages of WWII, *Belfast* would probably have been scrapped. (*D K Brown*)

3 | ARCTIC CONVOYS

NEARLY THREE YEARS WERE TO ELAPSE BEFORE *Belfast* rejoined the Fleet on 3 November 1942 under the command of Captain Frederick Parham. The pace of her reconstruction had been slowed by the removal of equipment and diversion of manpower to speed up the repairs of other ships which could be sent back into battle more swiftly. The dockyard began by rebuilding the hull's midships section and fitting splint-like reinforcing metal work beneath the enlarged armour belt. Bulges were fitted below the waterline to preserve her stability by countering the weight of this additional material, and increased her beam to 69ft. Although this work reduced her top speed to 30.5 knots, her capabilities were significantly enhanced by the installation of the latest air warning, surface warning and gunnery control radar equipment, as well as an improved anti-aircraft armament of five twin and eight single 20mm Oerlikon guns.

Belfast resumed her wartime career as flagship of the 10th Cruiser Squadron. Wearing the flag of Rear Admiral Robert Burnett, CB, OBE, she was assigned to protect the Arctic convoys which delivered tanks, aircraft, ammunition and other valuable items to resupply the Soviet forces fighting the Germans on the Eastern Front. Those who participated in these perilous voyages had to take on Mother Nature in a battle that was just as fierce as the frequent attacks by German submarines, aircraft and surface raiders. The horrific weather conditions included mountainous seas with

the power to rip off the top of a cruiser's turret, storm-force winds, freezing spray, blizzards, fog and temperatures as low as -30°C. The unimaginable misery of these conditions was compounded by the hazardous task of preventing the build-up of ice on the upper works, which could capsize a ship if left unchecked. Those who survived the ordeal of this treacherous journey to the Soviet Union received a welcome that matched the polar conditions from the very people they had risked their lives to help.

Despite the scale of the environmental challenge posed by navigating these hostile waters in the winter months, the long hours of darkness provided the convoys with a high degree of protection from an enemy attack. However, the winter's advancing pack ice forced the ships to pass to the south of Bear Island, which brought them within striking range of the Norwegian-based German forces. During this phase of each convoy's passage, the destroyer escort was strengthened by the close support of a cruiser force and the distant cover of at least one Home Fleet battleship. As summer approached, the lengthening hours of daylight significantly increased the risk of a German attack, which contributed to the suspension of the Arctic convoys between March and November 1943. Thus, following her involvement in the protection of the Arctic convoys JW53 and RA53, *Belfast* spent the summer months almost continuously engaged on patrols, blockade duties, offensive sorties and diver-

The sheer horror of the conditions endured by those who served in *Belfast* while escorting the Arctic convoys is graphically illustrated by this view of Able Seaman Thomas B Day standing against the cruiser's ice encrusted barbette for 'B' turret in November 1943. *(© Imperial War Museum, A20689)*

sionary sweeps in northern waters. A notable exception to this gruelling routine occurred on 15 August 1943 when King George VI inspected the ship's company during His Majesty's visit to the Home Fleet in Scapa Flow. Having received advance warning of the King's visit, Admiral Burnett ensured his flagship received a fresh coat of paint, in contrast to the Fleet's other weather-beaten ships, which caught His Majesty's attention and resulted in her becoming known as 'Tiddley B'.

4 | THE BATTLE OF NORTH CAPE

THE REDEPLOYMENT OF *LUTZOW* AND

Nürnberg to the Baltic, along with the disabling of *Tirpitz* by midget submarines, significantly altered the strategic picture during the suspension of the Arctic convoys in the summer of 1943. However, Germany's sole remaining operational major warship in Norwegian waters, *Scharnhorst*, still posed a serious threat when the convoys resumed in November 1943. The German Naval War Staff initially decided against using *Scharnhorst* to attack the convoys, because they feared that the Royal Navy's more effective radar could prove decisive in an engagement during the almost perpetual darkness of the Arctic winter. However, by late December, with the successful passage of three eastbound and two westbound convoys, political considerations became more pressing as the C-in-C of the German Navy, Grand Admiral Dönitz, needed to prove the continued importance of *Scharnhorst* to a sceptical Hitler. To achieve this, Dönitz decided to deploy the battlecruiser against the next Arctic convoy.

This fateful decision would bring *Scharnhorst* into conflict with the two groups of warships from the Home Fleet that had been assigned to reinforce the convoy's close protection within the vicinity of Bear Island. Wearing the flag of the recently promoted Vice Admiral Robert Burnett, *Belfast* led the cruisers of Force One, while Force Two was under the personal command of the C-in-C Home Fleet, Admiral Sir Bruce Fraser, KCB, KBE, in the battleship *Duke of York*. Having covered the east- and westbound convoys in the first half of December 1943, Force One stopped at Kola Inlet to take on fuel, while Force Two called in at Akureyri. Following their brief stopovers, both forces sailed on 23 December to cover the next pair of convoys (JW55B & RA55A). JW55B was detected by the Germans, who began to shadow it with aircraft and U-boats shortly after its departure from Loch Ewe on 20 December. Believing that the convoy's protection would not be reinforced by a British battleship, the German Naval War Staff issued orders to Rear Admiral Erich Bey in *Scharnhorst* on 25 December. The battlecruiser was to leave her Norwegian base and intercept the convoy off North Cape at first light the following morning. In the event of an enemy capital ship appearing, *Scharnhorst* was to withdraw immediately.

Admiral Fraser received confirmation of *Scharnhorst*'s departure from the Admiralty at 0339 on 26 December. The constant surveillance of JW55B by the Germans led Admiral Fraser to believe that *Scharnhorst* would attack this convoy rather than the westbound convoy. By 0400, JW55B was 50 miles south of Bear Island, while Force One was 150 miles to the east of JW55B and Force Two was 210 miles to the southwest. To frustrate Admiral Bey's efforts in locating the convoy, Admiral Fraser diverted JW55B to the north and ordered Admiral Burnett's cruisers to close the convoy for mutual support. Admiral Fraser hoped this would buy him valuable time to close in with *Duke of York* and bring *Scharnhorst* to action.

As the opposing forces steamed towards JW55B, *Belfast* made first contact with *Scharnhorst* at 0840 when her radar placed the battlecruiser between the convoy and Force One. As the gap continued to close, *Sheffield* caught sight of *Scharnhorst* at 0921 and three minutes later *Belfast* opened fire with starshell prior to Admiral Burnett ordering his cruisers to engage with their main armament. In the ensuing brief engagement, *Norfolk* scored one hit before the battlecruiser managed to use her greater speed to open up the range again and attempt to attack the convoy from the north. Realising Admiral Bey's intentions, Admiral Burnett turned his cruisers to keep them between *Scharnhorst* and JW55B, but lost radar contact with the enemy in the process.

Admiral Burnett's instincts were proved correct when *Belfast* regained radar contact at 1205. *Sheffield* once more established visual contact at 1221 and the cruisers immediately opened fire at a range of 11,000 yards. Meanwhile, the destroyers manoeuvred into position to launch a torpedo strike which was frustrated by the weather conditions and *Scharnhorst*'s rapid retirement. Although the cruisers claimed several hits, *Scharnhorst* inflicted serious damage on *Norfolk* with two direct hits on 'X' turret and the disabling of her radar.

As Admiral Bey withdrew from his encounter with Admiral Burnett's cruisers he decided to abort his plans and return to Norway. This placed her on a favourable intercept course with Force Two, enabling Admiral Burnett to shadow the battlecruiser and report her movements to Admiral Fraser. As the two groups continued to converge, *Scharnhorst* was

A reconstruction of *Belfast*'s initial engagement with *Scharnhorst* during the Battle of North Cape on 26 December 1943. *Belfast* has just fired a star-shell which illuminated the German warship in the far distance and she is about to unleash a broadside against her more heavily armed adversary. The splash of water in the foreground shows that *Belfast* is already coming under German fire. (© *Imperial War Museum, Art. IWM ART LD 7425)*

detected by *Duke of York*'s radar at a range of 45,500 yards at 1617. Half an hour later, *Belfast* opened the third engagement with starshell which failed to illuminate the target because of the range. However, *Duke of York*'s starshell proved more successful a minute later, enabling her to open fire with her main armament at a range of 12,000 yards at 1650. The battleship's presence came as a severe shock to those onboard *Scharnhorst* who had failed to detect *Duke of York*'s approach by radar. *Scharnhorst* responded by heading north and then east, pursued by Force Two. To prevent her escape to the north, *Belfast* and *Norfolk* opened fire until *Scharnhorst* was out of range at 1712. Pursued by the British warships, Admiral Bey headed east in a final attempt to outrun his hunters and opened up the gap to 18,000 yards, thereby placing her beyond the range of the cruisers' guns. However, the two capital ships continued to exchange fire, with *Duke of York* scoring a direct hit on *Scharnhorst*'s number one boiler room at 1820, which caused a drop in the battlecruiser's speed. Seizing their opportunity, Force Two's destroyers launched a torpedo attack resulting in three direct hits, including one that hit a boiler room and damaged a shaft to further reduce the battlecruiser's speed to 22 knots.

These hits proved decisive because they enabled Admiral Fraser to significantly reduce the gap and re-

engage *Scharnhorst* at a range of 10,400 yards with *Duke of York* and *Jamaica* at 1901. They immediately scored direct hits, which triggered a series of fires and explosions that took hold onboard the doomed battlecruiser while her speed dropped from 20 to 5 knots. *Scharnhorst*'s main armament only provided an intermittent return of fire with 'A' turret out of action and 'B' turret severely damaged. At 1915 *Belfast* rejoined the action to score a further two hits, before being ordered along with *Jamaica* to sink the almost stationary *Scharnhorst* with torpedoes. After their first attack the two cruisers were joined by the four destroyers attached to Force One, which launched a further assault before *Jamaica* delivered her second strike at 1937. Seven of these torpedoes fatally wounded the battlecruiser, and by the time *Belfast* approached to make her second attack at 1948 *Scharnhorst* had sunk. Despite an extensive search of the debris-strewn icy waters by *Belfast*, *Norfolk* and the destroyers, only thirty-six ratings from her ship's company of 1,970 men were rescued. Although the damaged *Tirpitz* continued to pose a potentially serious threat, the destruction of *Scharnhorst* removed the most immediate danger to the Arctic convoys.

From a historical point of view, this epic sea battle is important because it was the first to be determined by the use of radar and the last occasion on which a Royal Navy battleship engaged another capital ship.

Belfast's starboard side 4in guns open fire on German
shore positions in Normandy on the night of 27 June 1945.
(© Imperial War Museum, A24325)

5 | OPERATION TUNGSTEN

IN MARCH 1944, THE ADMIRALTY RECEIVED reports that the repairs to Germany's sole remaining capital ship, *Tirpitz*, were nearing completion in Altenfjord, northern Norway. To counter the renewed threat posed by the battleship, Admiral Fraser entrusted his second-in-command, Vice Admiral Sir Henry Moore, KCB, CVO, DSO, with the planning of an attack by carrier-borne bombers during the passage of the next outward-bound Arctic convoy JW58.

Belfast sailed from Scapa Flow as part of Admiral Fraser's heavy ship cover for JW58 on 30 March. A second group of ships, which would also form part of the attacking force, left Scapa Flow that evening under the command of Rear Admiral A W La Touche Bisset to head for a rendezvous point with Fraser's ships, approximately 250 miles northwest of Altenfjord, on 3 April. Once it became clear to Admiral Fraser that JW58's close escort did not require any reinforcement, he brought forward the timing of the attack by twenty-four hours to take advantage of a favourable spell of weather. When the two groups converged, *Anson, Victorious* and *Belfast* left Fraser's group to join the attacking force under the command of Admiral Moore in the battleship *Anson*. Admiral Fraser left the attacking force in his flagship *Duke of York* together with two destroyers, and headed towards a covering position to the northwest of Bear Island.

By 0437 on 3 April, the first strike force of twenty-one Barracudas had formed up with its fighter escort, consisting of twelve Corsairs, ten Hellcats, and twenty Wildcats, to begin the 120-mile journey to *Tirpitz*. A second group of twenty-one Barracudas followed nearly an hour later. The initial assault caught the German battleship by surprise as she was preparing to leave for sea trials, and achieved nine hits. The second strike achieved a further five hits. The combined effect of both attacks caused 122 deaths and 316 casualties onboard *Tirpitz*, which was disabled for another three months. Admiral Moore scrapped his plans for a second wave of attacks the following morning due to the level of damage that had been inflicted, and returned to Scapa Flow on 6 April. Eleven days later *Belfast* entered Rosyth for a brief refit, before sailing to Scapa Flow in time for King George VI's visit to the Home Fleet on 15 May.

6 | D-DAY LANDINGS

BELFAST CONCLUDED HER INVOLVEMENT WITHIN the European theatre of World War II by bombarding German forces during the initial stages of Operation Overlord – the code name adopted for the Allied invasion of France. The naval component of Overlord, Operation Neptune, involved 1,213 warships along with 4,126 landing ships and landing craft during the assault phase. *Belfast* was allocated to Bombardment Force E of the Eastern Task Force as the flagship of Rear Admiral Frederick Dalrymple-Hamilton, CB. Her role would be to disable the coastal defence battery of four 5.9in howitzers at Ver-sur-Mer in the two hours prior to the main assault on 6 June, before supporting the British and Canadian landings on Juno and Gold beaches. Afterwards, she was to deliver additional fire support as required by the advancing Allied ground forces, until the enemy lines were beyond the range of her main armament.

To prepare her ship's company for this assignment, *Belfast* joined the Royal Navy's other bombarding ships on the Clyde at the end of May 1944 for special training. Meanwhile, in London the cruiser became the subject of delicate discussions involving King George VI and Winston Churchill. During their weekly lunch on 30 May 1944, the King asked Winston Churchill where he planned to be on D-Day. The Prime Minister explained that he intended to watch the bombardment from HMS *Belfast*. As a former serving naval officer who had been present at the Battle of Jutland, His Majesty could not resist the temptation of joining his Prime Minister for a grandstand view of the greatest amphibious assault in history. However, their senior officials were horrified by the prospect of both men unnecessarily running the risk of being onboard a major warship that would have to run the gauntlet of mines, torpedoes, air attacks and shore batteries in return for a distant view of the action. Faced with these indisputable facts, His Majesty acknowledged his courtiers' concerns the following morning by cancelling his visit to *Belfast*. The King subsequently played a pivotal role in convincing Churchill to rearrange his own plans for D-Day, thereby saving Captain Parham the unenviable burden of ensuring the safety of both his Sovereign and Prime Minister in the heat of battle.

Back on the Clyde, *Belfast* sailed with the other bombarding ships on 2 June to ensure that she reached her designated position off the Normandy beaches three days later. However, poor weather forced the Supreme Allied Commander, General Eisenhower, to postpone the invasion by twenty-four hours. On receiving this signal, the bombarding ships reversed their course for twelve hours before heading south again. On 6 June the ship's company went to action stations in the early hours of the morning as the cruiser approached the French coast. At 0527 *Belfast* opened fire with a full broadside to port to begin two hours of continuous bombardment. When the Green Howards reached the battery at Ver-sur-Mer later that morning, they discovered that *Belfast* had knocked out the guns, and the German troops who

had manned the weapons were sheltering in their bunkers. Between 6 and 14 June *Belfast* fired 1,996 6in rounds at shore targets.

As the Allied troops advanced inland, *Belfast* supported the 3rd Canadian Division at Courcelles and the Royal Marine Commandos at Port-en-Bessin. On 8 July, she participated in the preparations for General Montgomery's breakout from Caen alongside the battleship *Rodney*, the monitor *Roberts* and the cruiser *Emerald*. Two days later the Allied forces had advanced beyond the range of *Belfast*'s main armament, thereby bringing her bombardment duties off the French coast to a close. She could now be released for service in the British Pacific Fleet and sailed north to be refitted by the Middle Docks Co on the Tyne from 4 August 1944 to 17 April 1945.

7 | FAR EAST PEACE-KEEPING DUTIES 1945–1950

THE EUROPEAN WAR WAS DRAWING TO A CLOSE by the time *Belfast* emerged from her Tyneside refit under the command of Captain R M Dick, CBE, DSC, RN. To prepare for the challenges of the Pacific theatre, the cruiser's close-range anti-aircraft armament had been increased to a strength of sixteen 2pdr pom-poms, split between four quadruple mountings, and twenty-six 20mm Oerlikons spread across twelve twin mountings and two single mountings. To compensate for the additional top weight incurred by these changes, the aft pair of 4in gun turrets were removed and replaced by extra accommodation. The redundant hangers were converted into accommodation, while the former flight deck became home to the ship's numerous boats and the sole remaining electric seaplane crane.

On completion of trials and exercises, *Belfast* sailed for the Far East on 17 June 1945 to become the flagship of the British Pacific Fleet's (BPF) 2nd Cruiser Squadron. However, the dropping of the atomic bombs on Hiroshima and Nagasaki brought the conflict to a close before she reached Sydney on 21 August. With the cessation of hostilities, the BPF's focus switched to accepting the surrender of Japanese forces across the region and dealing with rogue enemy units, followed by general peacekeeping duties, along with the repatriation of the former Allied prisoners of war and civilian internees.

In Sydney the ship's company embarked Australian Red Cross supplies for the liberated Allied prisoners in Formosa (Taiwan) and Shanghai. An impending typhoon curtailed *Belfast*'s Formosa visit. Thus she had to await the arrival of the other British and American warships of Task Group 11.3 off the Yangtze Bar before proceeding upstream to Shanghai on 19 September. Approximately four miles from Shanghai, the first group of former prisoners were spotted ashore standing around a flagpole flying the Union flag. The captain responded by sounding the ship's siren before the Royal Marine band on the quarterdeck struck up 'Here We Are Again'. *Belfast* spent the next four months transporting former prisoners from Shanghai to Hong Kong.

From January 1946 onwards, *Belfast*'s principal mission was to help counter the rising tension in the Far East by conducting goodwill visits to New Zealand, Fiji, Japan, China, North Borneo, and the Philippines. The commission concluded when she returned to Portsmouth on 15 October 1947 to pay off for a long refit.

Belfast recommissioned on 22 September 1948, under the command of Captain E K Le Mesurier, MVO, RN, for further service in the Far East where she would relieve HMS *Sussex* as flagship of the 5th Cruiser Squadron. Before commencing the two-month long voyage to Hong Kong, the cruiser briefly returned to

Belfast prepares to sail for the Far East in October 1948 to relieve HMS *Sussex* as flagship of the 5th Cruiser Squadron. However, prior to *Belfast's* departure from home waters, she briefly returned to her namesake city to accept the magnificent silver bell which can still be seen on the quarterdeck. Before the cruiser reached home waters again, she was to become embroiled in another conflict following the unprovoked invasion of South Korea by North Korean troops on 25 June 1950. (*Maritime Photo Library*)

her birthplace to be presented with the magnificent silver bell that can still be seen on her quarterdeck. By late December *Belfast* had reached Hong Kong. During her absence from the Far East, the tension had continued to rise across the region, including China, where the bitter civil war was reaching its climax as the Communist forces of Mao Tse-tung gained the upper hand over Chiang Kai-shek's Nationalists.

Belfast's New Year began with a covert mission to Chinese territory to retrieve a Royal Air Force Vampire which made an emergency landing on Tai Pang Wan beach on 12 January 1949. Once a salvage team from *Belfast* had successfully loaded the jet on to a pontoon, it was towed out into Bias Bay by some of the ship's boats and loaded on to the waiting cruiser.

Four months later, *Belfast* played a key, yet distant, role in the Yangtze Incident as the flagship of the C-in-C Far East Station, Admiral Sir Patrick Brind, KCB, CBE. In the autumn of 1948 the Chinese National Government had granted permission for the Royal Navy to resume the practice of stationing a guard ship at Nanking to support the British Embassy and safe-guard Commonwealth nationals. By April 1949, Mao Tse-tung's Chinese People's Liberation Army had reached the northern bank of the Yangtze and issued an ultimatum to its opponent. The Communists threat-ened to launch a full-scale offensive against the Nationalists on 21 April, unless they agreed to an

unopposed crossing of the Yangtze by 20 April. Admiral Brind's deputy, Vice Admiral A C G Madden, decided to take advantage of the temporary lull in fighting between the opposing Chinese forces to replace the destroyer *Consort* with the frigate *Amethyst* as Nanking's guard ship. In these circum-stances, the exchange of ships should have been a straightforward procedure. However, the Communist shore batteries opened fire on *Amethyst* as she steamed towards Nanking on 20 April. The attacks temporarily disabled the frigate and resulted in the death of nineteen men, including her commanding officer, Lt Cdr B M Skinner. Rescue attempts by the cruiser *London*, the frigate *Black Swan*, and *Consort* all ended in failure with heavy loss of life and casualties, due to further attacks by Communist forces which blockaded the stranded frigate for one hundred days.

During the stand-off, Admiral Brind established contact with *Amethyst's* new commanding officer, Lt Cdr Kerans, and encouraged him to break out. On the night of *Amethyst's* escape, Admiral Brind held a dinner party as planned in *Belfast* while secured to a mooring buoy over five hundred miles away in Hong Kong. As soon as the guests departed, the Admiral's dining room table was cleared to enable Sir Patrick to keep track of the latest developments, which culmi-nated the next morning with Kerans' signal, 'Have rejoined the Fleet. Am south of Woosung. No damage or casualties. God save the King.' *Belfast* remained on standby for several weeks as the Communist forces crossed the Yangtze River, in case British nationals had to be evacuated from the area.

Further drama occurred on the night of 31 October/ 1 November 1949 when *Belfast* rescued 226 passen- gers from the Nationalist tank-landing ship *Cheung Hsai*, which had run aground on the Pratas Reef in the South China Sea. The cruiser spent the beginning of 1950 undergoing a short refit in Singapore before embarking on the Far East Fleet's annual summer cruise on 12 May 1950.

8 | THE KOREAN WAR 1950-1952

WEARING THE FLAG OF FLAG OFFICER SECOND- in-Command Far East Station, Rear Admiral William Andrewes, CB, DSO, *Belfast* entered the Japanese port of Hakodate on 24 June 1950 as part of the Far East Fleet's summer cruise, which had been arranged to give the personnel a brief respite from the heat of Hong Kong and Singapore. On arrival it looked as though the potential track of Typhoon Elsie might disrupt the cruiser's immediate programme, so she was kept at a reduced notice of steam. However, much stronger winds of destruction were unleashed by the following morning's invasion of South Korea by the Communist state of North Korea. In view of the likely consequences of this unprovoked aggression, *Belfast* sailed from Hakodate that night, to enable Admiral Andrewes to discuss the situation in person with the US Navy's commander in Japan, Vice Admiral C T Joy, in Tokyo. As *Belfast* steamed south, the admiral received a signal from his superior, Admiral Sir Patrick Brind, warning that British ships might be required to act under the United Nations Charter.

The UN Security Council reacted swiftly by passing a resolution condemning the invasion on 25 June. A second resolution followed two days later, autho- rising the UN's members to assist South Korea's efforts to repel the Communist forces to the 38th parallel which forms the border between the Korean penin- sula's two countries. These resolutions were reinforced shortly afterwards by President Truman's announce- ment that American ships and aircraft would be deployed in support of the expulsion of North Korean forces from South Korea. Thirty other nations endorsed the President's policy, including the UK, which put the Royal Navy's warships in Japanese waters at Admiral Joy's disposal.

Belfast was initially assigned to Task Force 77 of the United States Seventh Fleet. Following its assembly in Okinawa, the joint Anglo-American group sailed for the Yellow Sea. As the task force approached the war zone at 20 knots, the staff officers continued to fine-

Memories of the WWII Arctic Convoys were revived by the winter gales, snow, ice floes and temperatures of -11°C that were endured by the ship's company while operating off the Korean west coast in February 1951. During her second west coast patrol of the month, *Belfast* steamed through miles of pack ice to bombard enemy positions as part of the Allied diversionary landings in the Taedong Estuary. (*James Payne/ www.throughtheireyes 2.co.uk*)

tune the plans for the forthcoming attacks, which kept the helicopters of the American carrier *Valley Forge* fully occupied transferring personnel between ships and delivering the latest despatches. On 3 and 4 July the carriers USS *Valley Forge* and HMS *Triumph* launched a series of air strikes against the airfields at Pyongyang and Haeju, as well as nearby railway infrastructure and North Korean troops. On conclusion of these attacks, the British warships, with the notable exception of *Triumph*, parted company from the Americans and sailed for the Japanese base of Sasebo, which became *Belfast*'s principal base for the duration of her Korean War service.

Meanwhile, President Truman issued orders on 4 July to impose a naval blockade of Korea. This led to the deployment of American warships along the east coast and patrols of the west coast by British, Commonwealth and Allied warships. *Belfast*, together with the destroyers *Cossack* and *Consort*, sailed five days later to conduct the inaugural west coast patrol. At night the ships hunted for blockade runners using the main shipping lanes between Korean and Chinese ports. By dawn the ships would loiter off one of the Korean ports before spending the day searching for junk traffic. Their repeated sweeps of these waters failed to provide any evidence of blockade runners, while the intercepted junks consisted of harmless fishing boats and those transporting refugees from the occupied territories.

Following her relief by *Jamaica* on 15 July, *Belfast* was assigned to the American forces for five days of bombardment duties along the east coast in which she fired 752 6in shells. The targets included barracks, factories, roads, railways, bridges, and the town of Yong Dok prior to the US Army's successful assault. British and American aircraft provided aerial spotting for the bulk of the shoots, although ground observers occasionally performed the role. The accuracy of her gun crews earned high praise from the American commander of the East Coast Support Group, Rear Admiral J M Higgins, who described *Belfast* as 'that straight-shooting ship'.

Belfast concluded her first Korean tour of duty by undertaking a second west coast patrol at the end of July and firing 252 rounds of 6in shells on 5 August while bombarding Inchon's oil storage facilities, factories, warehouses, and gun positions. A day later *Belfast* returned to Sasebo to disembark Admiral Andrewes and his staff before setting sail for Chatham Dockyard, where she arrived on 9 October. The cruiser remained in the UK for just seventeen days, in which time she recommissioned with a full wartime complement, before returning for her second tour of duty off the Korean coast.

At her standard displacement of 11,550 tons, *Belfast* drew 18ft 3in forward which increased to 22ft 3¾in when she reached her deep load displacement of 14,325 tons. In this head-on view of *Belfast,* during a brief docking period in the Japanese port of Kure in October 1951, the underwater profile of two bulges that were added during the 1940–42 reconstruction can be clearly seen along with the crisp outline of the knuckle which provides a sharp contrast to the elegant flared profile of the lower half of the hull above the waterline. (*James Payne/www.throughtheireyes2.co.uk*)

During her absence, the Chinese Army had entered the conflict on the North Korean side and was fighting the UN forces to the south of Seoul by the time *Belfast* sailed from Sasebo on 2 February 1951 to conduct her first west coast patrol of the year. Seventeen days later *Belfast* sailed round to the east coast to participate in the siege of Wonsan, and bombarding the nearby island of Sin Do before the South Korean Marines launched a successful assault. At the beginning of March, she reverted to the west coast and took part in the diversionary landings in the Taedong Estuary. On reaching the mouth of the estuary, the cruiser bombarded enemy positions in an operation that involved the expenditure of 410 rounds of 6in, 217 rounds of 4in and twenty-four rounds of starshell ammunition.

Although helicopters were never permanently embarked in *Belfast*, they could land on the quarterdeck following the lowering of the ensign staff and guardrails, and training 'Y' turret abeam. During the Korean War, USN Sikorsky HO3S-1s like this were frequent visitors to the ship bringing urgent dispatches, flag officers and other dignitaries. While conducting an exercise with the carrier USS *Yorktown* at the end of June 1960, *Belfast*'s Chinese barber, Lai Sum, was suddenly taken ill with an internal haemorrhage. The ship immediately altered course for Okinawa and was met on route by a USN Sikorsky H34 Seabat, which became the largest helicopter to land on the quarterdeck when it arrived to transfer the patient to Okinawa's American military hospital, where he made a full recovery. *(James Payne/ www.throughtheireyes2.co.uk)*

Rear Admiral A K Scott-Moncrieff, CB, DSO*, succeeded Admiral Andrewes on 10 April, and *Belfast* completed one more west coast patrol, prior to entering Singapore in May for a brief refit which included the replacement of all her 6in barrels. *Belfast*'s return to the war zone on 1 September proved to be the start of the busiest three months of her Korean War service consisting of five west coast patrols and two deployments to the east coast. At the end of September *Belfast* supported the amphibious assault on Wonsan by 41 Commando Royal Marines, followed in mid October by a major attack on the town of Kojo, in which the cruiser fired 529 rounds of 6in.

The ship's company faced another challenge from Mother Nature when *Belfast* sailed from Sasebo on 14 October to ride out Typhoon Ruth in the relative safety of the open sea. Conditions deteriorated throughout the day and the cruiser was forced to heave to in the afternoon when 6in shells broke loose in one of the shell rooms. That night she heaved to again to ride out the worst as the centre of the typhoon passed within 110 miles of the ship. The wave crests exceeded the height of the flag deck and the ship rolled up to 35 degrees while the seas filled the waists to a depth of four feet. Not surprisingly, there was a lot of damage to the external fittings, including the loss of seven Carley floats and the starboard lower boom.

She spent the beginning of November on the west coast where she led an unsuccessful attempt to eliminate enemy batteries on the Amgak peninsula. On 20 and 21 November, she participated in the attack of Hungnam as the senior ship of the international Task Group 95.8, which included the Australian carrier

HMAS *Sydney*, along with destroyers from the British, Canadian, Australian, Dutch, and American navies. On completion of this raid, she sailed for Yokosuka where Captain Duckworth, DSO, DSC, RN, relieved Captain Sir Aubrey St Clair-Ford, DSO*, RN, on 23 November, at the beginning of a month's break from operations in which the ship's company celebrated Christmas early in Hong Kong.

Thus *Belfast* spent Christmas and New Year bombarding batteries on the Amgak peninsula. Between mid January and late September 1952, *Belfast* undertook a further eighteen west coast patrols. Notable events included the cruiser's participation in the recapture of the island of Changni-do on 16 July and sustaining a direct hit while bombarding a battery on the island of Wolsa-ri during her penultimate patrol on 29 July. Remarkably, it was the only occasion on which she was hit by enemy gunfire throughout the Korean War, despite regularly steaming within range of North Korean shore batteries. Sadly, the 76mm shell penetrated the starboard side and fractured a steam pipe which killed Leading Steward Lau So and injured four other Chinese ratings.

The conclusion of *Belfast*'s final patrol on 27 September 1952 brought her involvement in the Korean War to a close. Since June 1950 she had spent 404 days on patrol, steamed in excess of 97,000 miles and bombarded enemy positions with over 8,000 6in rounds – more than she had fired throughout WWII. Although the conflict continued until 27 July 1953, *Belfast* returned to Chatham Dockyard where she paid off on 4 November 1952 and was accepted into Class III reserve at Devonport Dockyard on 1 December 1952. Her immediate prospects looked bleak as once more her fate hung in the balance.

9 | FINAL COMMISSIONS 1956-1963

IT TOOK THE ADMIRALTY OVER TWO YEARS TO decide whether *Belfast* should be modernised or consigned to the scrapheap. Fortunately, the Navy still required a small number of cruisers to act as flagships on foreign stations, therefore the Board of Admiralty granted the middle-aged cruiser a reprieve in March 1955 by approving plans for her modernisation. The subsequent work, carried out in Devonport Dockyard between January 1956 and May 1959, significantly altered *Belfast*'s external profile with the addition of an enclosed bridge, lattice masts, and a revised close-range armament of six twin 40mm Bofors guns. The removal of the torpedo armament reduced top weight and freed up valuable internal space for other purposes. The living conditions for the enlarged ship's company of 956 men were transformed by the introduction of centralised messing and the provision of centralised air conditioning throughout the ship, which could handle tropical conditions as well as atomic, biological and chemical warfare.

Belfast recommissioned in Devonport Dockyard on 12 May 1959 under the command of Captain John Wilkinson, DSC, GM, RN. On completion of sea trials and preliminary exercises she sailed on 20 August for the Far East where she became the flagship of the Flag Officer Second-in-Command of the Far East Station, Rear Admiral Varyl Begg, CB, DSO, DSC. The year 1960 proved to be a busy one for the refurbished cruiser, in which she spent 210 days at sea, in between visits to Hong Kong, Borneo, India, Australia, South Korea, Japan and the Philippines. The year also marked the tenth anniversary of South Korea's invasion by North Korean troops. The Western powers viewed this milestone with apprehension, because they feared it could be used as an opportunity for renewed aggression by North Korea. In a bid to deter any sabre-rattling by the Communist regime, the South East Asia Treaty Organisation (SEATO) staged Exercise Sea Lion at the beginning of May, involving warships from the navies of the UK, America, France, Australia, New Zealand, Pakistan, Thailand, and the Philippines. At the end of the month, Admiral Begg took the fleet, including *Belfast*, to Inchon in a further show of force which helped to stem the increasing tension.

The cruiser's year concluded on a more peaceful note with a routine refit in Singapore before she paid off on 31 January 1961. The Admiralty decided to change over the ship's company from this commission with the men for the next one using Bristol Britannia airliners of the Royal Air Force Transport Command.

On completion of *Belfast*'s initial anchoring trials beyond Plymouth's breakwater on 3 June 1959, she anchored just inside the breakwater for the night. Afterwards, the port side accommodation ladder was lowered to provide a convenient method of joining or leaving the ship via a small boat while the lower boom enabled the ship's boats to lie clear of the hull when they were not in use. (*Maritime Photo Library*)

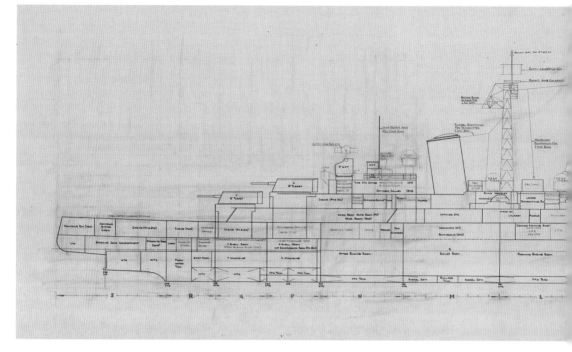

A total of eleven return flights were required to carry out the exchange, which took place over several weeks, thereby saving *Belfast* the four-month round trip between the UK and Singapore. On conclusion of the thanksgiving service for the old commission, *Belfast* recommissioned on the same day under the command of Captain Morgan Giles, DSO, OBE, GM, RN, who subsequently played a pivotal role in her preservation.

Once again *Belfast* served as the flagship of the Flag Officer Second-in-Command of the Far East Station for the majority of the commission, which began with Exercises Jet '61 and Pony Express. At the end of June preparations for a routine docking period in Singapore were interrupted by Iraq's threat to invade Kuwait, which had gained its independence from the UK two weeks earlier. The captain received orders to bring the cruiser to eight hours' notice of steam. The ship's company worked overnight to re-embark the stores and ammunition they had just unloaded, while the engineers reassembled the equipment on which they were about to start work. However, the expected call to arms never materialised, thanks to the rapid build-up of other British forces in the region including the carriers *Bulwark* and *Victorious* which diffused the immediate threat of invasion. Thus, after several days on standby, *Belfast* reverted to forty-eight hours' notice of steam and entered dry dock on 14 July as planned.

On completion of the docking period, *Belfast* sailed for the Coral Sea to participate in Exercise Tucker Box with the Royal Australian Navy, followed by goodwill visits to Melbourne and Sydney. Ceremonial events dominated the final two months of the year with a visit to Hong Kong in November for Remembrance Sunday and Princess Alexandra's review of the Fleet. Afterwards, *Belfast* crossed the Indian Ocean to the East African port of Dar-es-Salaam to play a prominent role in the independence of Tanganyika (Tanzania) on 8 December.

Belfast returned to Singapore for Christmas and the New Year before rounding off her Far East service with visits to the Philippines, Malaya, India and Ceylon, followed by the SEATO Exercise Jet '62. On 26 March 1962 she sailed from Singapore for the last time to begin the twelve-week long voyage back to Portsmouth via Hong Kong, Guam, Pearl Harbor, San Francisco, Seattle, Vancouver, Victoria, the Panama Canal, Trinidad, and Devonport, to conclude a commission in which she steamed 73,500 miles.

She recommissioned on 2 July 1962 for an eight-month commission with the Home Fleet, which included the firing of her last full broadside on 18 September, and a farewell visit to Belfast at the end of November. The lowering of her White Ensign on 25 February 1963 appeared to signal the end of *Belfast*'s seagoing career as she paid off into reserve. However, there was to be a brief swansong for the veteran cruiser thanks to the Admiral Commanding Reserves, Rear Admiral H C Martell, CB, CBE, who instigated *Belfast*'s final six-week commission under the command of Captain H C J Shand, DSC, RN. In contrast to her

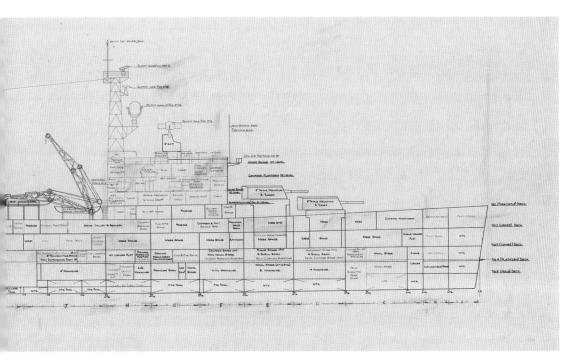

This 1956 profile provides quite a contrast to the original drawings (pages 8–9) from twenty years earlier, and illustrate the extent of *Belfast's* development during her time in commission. Red ink has been used to highlight some of the alterations that were due to be implemented during *Belfast's* forthcoming modernisation, including the construction of a new enclosed forward superstructure and the stepping of two new lattice masts. (© *National Maritime Museum, Greenwich, London, J8784*)

This close up of view of *Belfast's* amidships clearly shows many of the changes that were carried out during her 1956–59 modernisation including the fitting of inflatable life rafts, the enclosure of the previously open sections of 02 Deck and the packed boat deck. *Belfast's* arrival in Malta's Grand Harbour on 28 August 1959 signalled the beginning of an intensive four-week work-up for the ship's company which included anti-aircraft exercises using pilotless target aircraft as well as sleeve targets towed by Meteors from the nearby RAF base at Hal Far, 6in firings against sled targets, a dummy attack by frogmen, and night exercises. On completion of these procedures *Belfast* resumed her voyage to the Far East at the end of September. (*Anthony & Joseph Pavia/ National Museum of the Royal Navy*)

Belfast concluded her service in the Far East by participating in the South East Asia Treaty Organisation's (SEATO) Exercise Jet '62. The annual event took place in the Indian Ocean and on this occasion involved warships from the Indian, Australian, New Zealand, Malayan, Canadian and British navies. The programme consisted of anti-submarine, surface and carrier exercises as well as a rehearsal of atomic defence. *Belfast* is seen during the exercise while firing a 6in broadside off the Nicobar Islands. (© *Imperial War Museum, HU 4643*)

previous commissions, her ship's company consisted of officers and men of the Royal Naval Reserve together with three hundred Sea Cadets and seventy medical Sub Lieutenants. Wearing Rear Admiral Martell's flag, *Belfast* sailed from Portsmouth on 10 August 1963 with the entire 10th Minesweeping Squadron and steamed to Gibraltar for the two-week long Exercise Rockhaul. It proved to be an extremely useful deployment which enabled the participants to practise most aspects of

seamanship and several naval evolutions.

Having steamed nearly 500,000 miles, Belfast's active service drew to a close when Captain Shand brought her alongside in Devonport Dockyard for the last time on 24 August 1963 and gave the order 'Ring off main engines'. She then paid off into reserve and was subsequently transferred to Portsmouth where she became the Headquarters and Accommodation Ship of the Portsmouth Division of Reserve Ships in May 1966.

The Admiralty predicted that *Belfast*'s machinery could operate for at least another ten years following her 1956–59 modernisation. In the course of the two Far East commissions that followed this work, she clocked up another 133,500 miles before reverting to a more sedate pace in home waters for her final spell of active service. (*Tom Molland / Abrahams / World Ship Society*)

Following two active commissions in the Far East, *Belfast* recommissioned for further service in home waters under the command of Captain M G R Lumby, DSO, DSC, RN. Wearing the flag of Vice Admiral J G Hamilton, CB, CBE, Flag Officer Flotillas, Home Fleet, the recently recommissioned *Belfast* sails from Portsmouth in July 1962 to work up the new ship's company in preparation for the challenges of they might face in the commission ahead. (*Wright & Logan / National Museum of the Royal Navy*)

10 | PRESERVATION

THE RELEGATION OF A WARSHIP TO ACCOMMO-dation duties usually signals the beginning of the end. However, in the case of *Belfast*, it was to provide an opportunity to avoid the scrapman's blowtorch. The remarkable tale of her escape from destruction began on 14 April 1967 when a four-man team from the Imperial War Museum (IWM) visited HMS *Gambia* in Portsmouth Dockyard to inspect her main armament. The museum had previously preserved two 15in guns from the battleships *Ramillies* and *Resolution* as a reminder of the mighty dreadnoughts that once wore the White Ensign. Sadly, the dream of preserving an entire battleship proved unachievable in the UK, with proposals to save *Warspite* and *Vanguard* failing to gain enough momentum. In contrast, similar schemes in America have resulted in the preservation of eight battleships since 1948.

The situation didn't look any better as the Royal Navy prepared to dispose of its remaining wartime cruisers in the late 1960s. To mark the passing of the big-gun cruiser, the IWM decided to preserve a whole gun turret. Following their tour of *Gambia*, the museum's team were invited for lunch onboard HMS *Belfast*. As they left, Peter Simkins turned to his colleagues and suggested the idea of preserving an entire ship. To assess the scale of the challenge, the group liaised with those behind the preservation of

historic ships abroad, including four of the American battleships and the Russian cruiser *Aurora*. Their findings indicated that the potential costs were unlikely to be prohibitive. *Belfast* emerged as the best option, due to her good condition and distinguished naval career.

In November 1967 the IWM's trustees authorised the formation of a committee, led by its director, Dr Noble Frankland, to prepare detailed plans. Their subsequent report in June 1968 confirmed the viability of preserving *Belfast* in Portsmouth Dockyard. However, the government's refusal to pay for her to become a national museum in February 1971, followed by its decision to place *Belfast* on the disposal list, appeared to seal her fate. Undeterred by this dramatic turn of events, the scheme's influential supporters established the HMS *Belfast* Trust under the chairmanship of Rear Admiral Morgan-Giles who commanded the cruiser from 1961 to 1962 and was by then the MP for Winchester. The trust immediately began raising the required funding from private sources including the banker and former MP, John Smith, who donated £100,000. Admiral Morgan-Giles managed to secure a temporary stay of execution by raising the cruiser's plight in the House of Commons. This provided the new organisation with enough time to apply for charitable status, identify a suitable berth, and decide how to present her to the public. By gaining access to the

Time appeared to have finally run out for HMS *Belfast* in May 1971 when she was stripped of any remaining useful equipment and laid up in Fareham Creek to await her final voyage to the scrapyard. (*Maritime Photo Library*)

IWM's groundwork they had a tremendous head start, although they decided to switch the ship's proposed home from Portsmouth to London to benefit from the year-round flow of tourists. Hay's Wharf subsequently emerged as the best option due to the regeneration plans for the Pool of London and the constant flow of visitors to the nearby Tower of London.

The scheme, codenamed Operation Seahorse in honour of the ship's badge, was finally given the green light in June when the Government agreed to donate *Belfast* to the trust. Within three months she had been towed to Tilbury for conversion into a museum ship. Trafalgar Day, 21 October 1971, was chosen for the official opening thereby underlining her status as the first warship to be saved for the nation since Lord Nelson's flagship HMS *Victory* was preserved in 1922. To maintain as much of the cruiser's naval character as possible, the trust was granted permission for *Belfast* to wear the White Ensign and be styled Her Majesty's Ship.

The gamble paid off, with *Belfast* swiftly becoming a popular attraction and winning several tourist awards. The initial visitor route was progressively expanded throughout the 1970s as the Trust secured further practical and financial support to open up more compartments including the operations room, the forward steering position and the main galley, as well as the forward engine and boiler rooms. Even though *Belfast* had attracted 1,500,000 visitors by December 1975, the Trustees were still concerned about the future, not least having to cover the cost of dry docking the ship. To resolve the situation they sought the financial security offered by becoming part of the IWM. Reassured by the Trust's success, the Government approved the IWM's acquisition of the cruiser on 1 March 1978 to ensure her permanent preservation. This enabled the anticipated dry docking in Tilbury to go ahead in September 1982. A second dry docking period led to *Belfast*'s return to the sea for the first time in twenty-eight years when she was towed back to Portsmouth for a month's conservation work in June 1999. The subsequent inspection revealed that the hull was in remarkably good condition and did not require any plating work. Due to the

In a dramatic twist of fate, *Belfast* escaped the scrapman's blowtorch thanks to the efforts of the HMS *Belfast* Trust which raised enough money to refit and exhibit the veteran cruiser in the Pool of London. Thus, when she left Portsmouth under tow on 2 September 1971, it marked the beginning of a new chapter in her long and distinguished history rather than the beginning of the end. (*Maritime Photo Library*)

Belfast entered the King George V Dock, Woolwich on 4 October 1971 for ten days of work below the waterline prior to being towed up the Thames to her permanent moorings in the Pool of London. During this period she was inspected by the former Director of Naval Construction Sir Victor Shepheard. Afterwards, he confirmed that the hull was in superb condition and 'would last indefinitely.' *(© Imperial War Museum, MH 14570)*

To satisfy the legal requirement of declaring a consideration when transferring the ownership of a registered ship, the IWM handed over this £1 note to the HMS *Belfast* Trust in payment for the ship. Shortly afterwards, the Trust was disbanded although some of its officials, including Rear Admiral Morgan-Giles, continued their involvement with the ship's future as members of the HMS *Belfast* Advisory Board.

ship's static role, the IWM decided not to apply antifoul to the hull because the growth that had accumulated in the previous seventeen years was short and tightly packed. Instead, the IWM decided to apply the two-part epoxy mix Ameron PSX700 which should protect the hull below the waterline for at least

twenty-five years. Thus, unless any other problems come to light, *Belfast* is unlikely to be dry docked again until 2024.

Whilst the Government provides the ultimate safeguard for *Belfast*, the IWM must generate funding via the ship's facilities whenever possible. She attracts approximately 250,000 visitors every year and the income from their admission fees is supplemented by several sources including the onboard café, quayside gift shop and the private events organised by Sodexo Prestige. Another useful stream of money is generated by the sleepover programme which enables groups of up to 52 children aged 8–18 years and six adults to spend a maximum of three consecutive nights in two restored mess decks. The scheme attracts school children from across the UK who then visit some of London's other attractions during the day.

To ensure *Belfast* maintains her appeal as one of London's major tourist attractions the IWM regularly reviews the onboard displays. In recent years, this process, together with the IWM's education programme, has been assisted by the growing involvement of those who served in *Belfast* via the HMS

Despite a tongue-in-cheek explanation that the man at the top of the foremast was holding a hacksaw just in case the figures were wrong, *Belfast* actually passed below the upper works of Tower Bridge without any difficulties on 14 October 1971. Rather than forming part of any contingency plans, the man who had scaled the foremast was in fact a cameraman in search of an unusual angle to record a historic moment for posterity. (© *Imperial War Museum, MH 15062*)

Following a month's work in one of the Dockyard's dry docks, which included repainting the entire hull up to the upper deck, *Belfast* leaves Portsmouth under tow bound for her permanent moorings in the Pool of London in July 1999. (*Mike Lennon*)

Belfast Association. This organisation was formed as a result of a chance meeting of like-minded veterans in October 1998. The IWM has actively supported the association from the outset by providing its headquarters on board the ship and involving its members in every major event including the 1999 dry docking, the Thames Diamond Jubilee Pageant, and the celebrations to mark the 75th anniversary of her launch. In turn, the IWM has benefited from the relationship by having access to a unique source of information about virtually every aspect of the ship and her history.

Remarkably, *Belfast* is now in her fifth decade as a museum ship. Summing up the practical issues of caring for *Belfast,* the Conservation and Facilities Manager, Andy Curran, explained, 'Preserving *Belfast* in her present condition is a delicate balance, taking into account the safety of visitors and staff, the availability of appropriate materials and their fixings, the ability to use traditional methods of repair and cost. Another major factor is the need to create space for the administration of the ship. At present almost half the ship is open for public access and viewing. Areas which are not open are excluded for various reasons: difficult access, administrative use, educational use or corporate function use. Where possible, an example of each type of compartment has been made available for viewing. This is supplemented by a "virtual tour" sited on the main communications deck, which allows sight of ten inaccessible areas. Resources for the conservation of the ship are finite and a balance always has to be struck between restoration and maintenance.'

In terms of the wider lessons which can be learned from *Belfast's* successful preservation, she has proved that the permanent conservation of a large historic ship depends on a combination of factors including a long lead time to undertake the necessary research for the preparation of a realistic proposal; the financial backing of a major organisation (public or private) to cover any shortfalls in revenue or unforeseen expenses; a prominent display berth that attracts tourists throughout the year; a methodical long-term maintenance programme; the use of employed and volunteer staff; the ability to exploit any commercial opportunity whether it's establishing an onboard café or the vessel's use for corporate events; working with support groups of enthusiasts or veterans associated with the particular type of ship, and refreshing the ship's overall presentation on a regular basis. Equally, if there is a choice of more than one example of a particular type or class of ship, priority should be given to the vessel with the most exciting heritage and best structural condition. By understanding the impact of all these factors, those behind any future projects to save a large historic ship will stand a better chance of success.

THE HULL

The original profile of *Belfast*'s hull was significantly altered by the fitting of bulges either side below the main armour belt during her 1940–42 reconstruction.

Above: The way in which *Belfast* is presented has always been an issue as the most significant events of her naval career occurred before she underwent considerable changes during the 1956–59 modernisation. The clearest example of this dilemma is provided by the IWM's decision in 1993 to replace her straightforward post-war overall grey livery with the eye-catching Admiralty Disruptive Camouflage Type 25. Even though this scheme was applied to *Belfast* during WWII, it is, from a historical point of view, quite at odds with her otherwise Cold War era appearance.

Above right: The pronounced knuckle was designed to enable *Belfast* to maintain a higher speed in rough weather by deflecting the spray from the deck and increasing lift.

Bottom left: As part of *Belfast*'s 1940–42 reconstruction, a bulge was added either side of the hull to preserve the cruiser's stability following the addition of heavy new equipment together with all of the reinforcing metalwork that was used to repair the damage caused by the German magnetic mine. This close-up view clearly illustrates the contrast between the port side bulge and the crisp lines of the main armour belt.

Bottom right: The 6in high Roman numerals indicate the ship's draught. On some ships they would have been cut in by chisel or centre punch whereas metal figures were used for this purpose on *Belfast*'s hull. This image clearly shows that the cruiser currently draws 18ft because the waterline is along the lower edge of the Roman numerals XVIII.

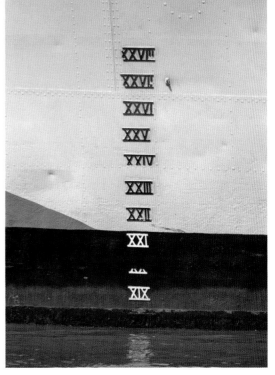

Above and right: The ship is moored alongside two large wooden dolphins that are secured to the river bed and are high enough to allow for a daily rise and fall of 20ft as the tides ebb and flood. During *Belfast*'s conversion at Tilbury, metal bearers were attached to the port side to act as the point of contact between the dolphins and the hull. Three strong chains attached to permanent moorings on the riverbed hold *Belfast*'s bow firmly in position against the combined effects of winds and of the river's tidal currents.

Below: The leading edges of the bulge added during *Belfast*'s 1940–42 reconstruction and the armour belt were faired in to the hull as much as possible to reduce the level of drag that they created as the ship sliced through the water.

Below: Although riveted construction was used to secure the majority of *Belfast's* steel plates to each other and the main structural members, welding was used in the construction of several sections of the ship including the lower stem. The thickness of the steel plates was determined by their position in the hull, with the strongest plates fitted along the bottom below the engine and boiler rooms. The ship's most important compartments such as the magazines, shell rooms and machinery were grouped as closely together as possible and protected by armour plating secured to the hull's outer surface. These 4½in thick slabs of specially toughened and hardened steel run from 3ft below the waterline to the upper deck level from a position immediately ahead of the forward boiler room to a point immediately astern of the aft engine room. Either side of these sections, the main armour belt extends at a lower level to a point immediately ahead of 'A' turret's shell room and to a point astern of 'Y' turret's shell room.

Belfast's principal statistics following her 1956–59 modernisation were as follows:

Overall length	613½ft
Maximum beam	69ft
Maximum draught	29½ft
Machinery	4 x Parsons geared turbines driving 4 shafts
Total shaft horsepower	80,000shp
Maximum speed	30 knots
Height of foremast	111ft
Standard displacement	11,550 tons
Full load displacement	14,930 tons
Armament	12 x 6in, 8 x 4in and 12 x 40mm Bofors
Complement	54 officers and 662 ratings

(Photograph taken by Julian Mannering)

Top left and right: *Befast* is the same length and weight as the Post Office Tower, and maintaining a historic ship of this size is a considerable task. On average it takes the conservation team two years to completely repaint the ship. There is no set schedule for this because it is influenced by factors such as the weather, the diversion of manpower to more pressing projects, and the availability of funds. The team also consider the timing of major events in the capital when planning the most visible elements of *Belfast*'s maintenance, so that she is not clad in scaffolding during high-profile occasions such as the Thames Diamond Jubilee Pageant held on 3 June 2012. *(Photographs taken by Julian Mannering)*

Above: A close-up view of the starboard side anchor, secured within the hawsepipe.

Below: Bathed in the early golden sunlight of a perfect summer's morning, a deserted *Belfast* awaits the next influx of visitors. *(Photograph taken by Julian Mannering)*

Left: A permanent gangway was constructed to provide access for visitors from The Queen's Walk to the port side of the Quarterdeck. The electricity cables that connect the ship to mains shore power are laid within enclosed channels that run along the edge of the gangway. Like the bow, *Belfast*'s stern is held firmly in place against the prevailing conditions by three strong anchor chains that are secured to permanent moorings on the riverbed. *(Photograph taken by Julian Mannering)*

Below: An extended landing platform was added to the stern on the starboard side during *Belfast*'s conversion into a museum ship at Tilbury during 1971, so that visitors could be brought to the ship by ferries or boats. When the ship's first Director, Vice Admiral Sir Donald Gibson, asked the contractor's foreman if he was happy with the strength of the welding to the armour plate, the foreman decided to demonstrate his faith in the quality of the work by hitting it with a mawl. Sadly, his confidence proved unfounded and the platform ended up in the bottom of the dry dock. Fortunately, the subsequent attempt to secure the platform to the ship's side has been more durable. During the summer months, visiting warships and cruise ships can often be seen moored alongside *Belfast*'s starboard side – this provides an additional stream of income from the Port of London Authority.

Above: To add to the sense of occasion during *Belfast*'s numerous overseas goodwill visits during her active career, the ship's side could be lit up at night by floodlights. They were mounted outboard of the hull on metal poles in a similar fashion to this fitting which is used to illuminate the original red lettering of the ship's name at the stern.

THE FORECASTLE

The term forecastle, always pronounced fo'c'sle, dates back to the Middle Ages when fighting ships were fitted with a raised structure over the bows and stern. Armed men would be stationed in these 'castles' to repulse boarders or attack the men on enemy ships. On *Belfast*, the term describes the forward section of 1 Deck where the anchor cables and shore lines were handled.

Above: This view clearly shows the route taken by the starboard side anchor cable from the hawse pipe to the cable holder, before it disappears below decks down the navel pipe to the cable locker in the fore-peak.

Top right: *Belfast* carried three 110cwt stockless anchors, consisting of two bower and one sheet, until June 1943 when the sheet anchor was landed to reduce the top weight. Although the sheet anchor's hawse pipe was blanked over at the same time, its position remained visible on the starboard bow until the last signs were removed during the 1956–59 modernisation.

Bottom right: The hand-operated wheels, mounted astern of the cable holders, controlled the brake, which governed the speed of the anchor cable when letting go of an anchor. Unlike the capstan, these cable holders could not be manually operated in the event of a mechanical failure. In such circumstances, the middle line capstan would have to be used to work the anchor cable.

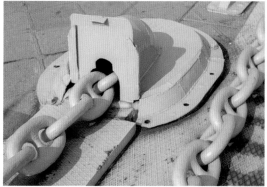

Top left: One of the anchor cables that forms part of *Belfast*'s permanent mooring arrangements runs up through the port side hawse pipe and is secured by a large shackle to another short length of chain that has been passed around the port side cable holder.

Middle left: The starboard side fairlead.

Bottom left: A single capstan is fitted along the forecastle's centre line between the two cable holders and would have been primarily used for hauling in shore lines while berthing. In the event of a mechanical failure, the capstan could be turned manually by inserting wooden bars into the slots at the top of the capstan. To raise an anchor in this manner would have been a major task and required the combined efforts of 144 men.

Above: The bonnet reduced the amount of water that could flood down the navel pipe to the cable locker in a rough sea.

Top right: One of the anchor cables which holds *Belfast* in position on the River Thames is secured to the starboard side bollard.

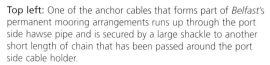

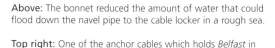

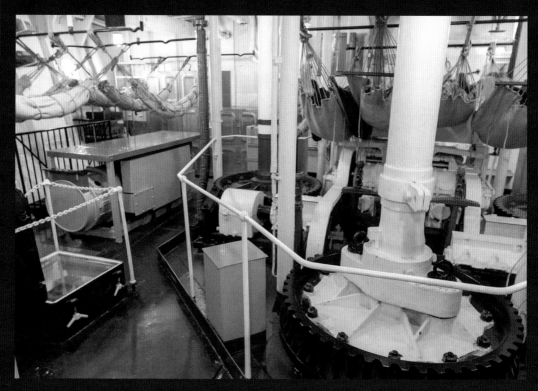

BELOW THE FORECASTLE

Above: Located immediately below the forecastle, the capstan machinery space is dominated by the large electric motor that drives the heavy-duty reduction gears connected to the cable holders and capstan. The red and green paint at the base of the two outboard shafts indicate which cable holder they are connected to, while black paint has been used to highlight the capstan's reduction gears and plain white for its shaft. This space also accommodated 33 sailors who had to sling their hammocks in between these large items of machinery. The open hatch, in the bottom left-hand corner of this image, leads down to the cable locker.

Right: Each anchor cable consisted of 425 fathoms (2550ft) of 2⅛in forged steel Admiralty quality chain. The unused section of the cable was stored in the cable locker in the fore-peak where the inboard end was secured via a senhouse slip to the cable clench. In this view the senhouse slip can be seen lying on the wooden planking which covers the starboard side cable locker. To reduce the prospect of the cable parting, the cable lockers would be emptied every six months and the cable ranged on deck for a thorough link-by-link inspection.

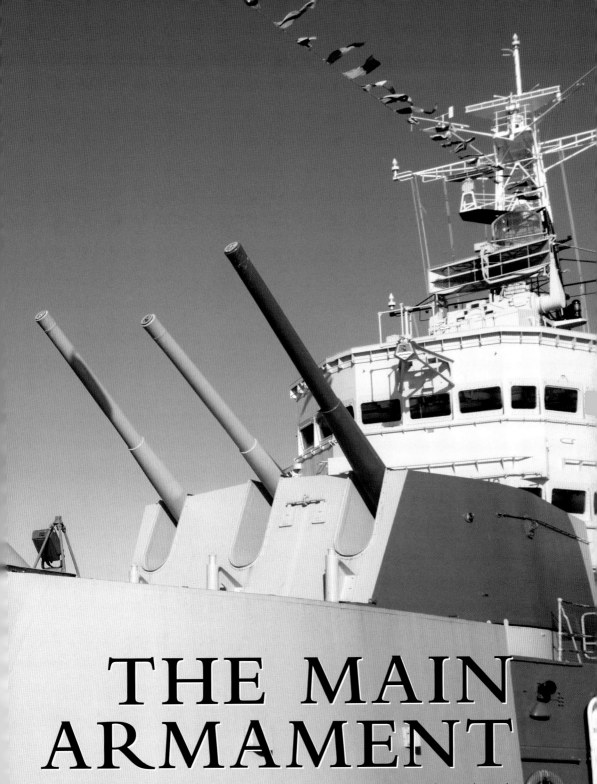

THE MAIN ARMAMENT

Belfast's powerful main armament consists of twelve 6in MkXXIII breech-loading guns, of the all-steel type, split between four triple MkXXIII mountings that could train up to 120° on either side of the centre line. Each turret weighs 175 tons and is identified by a letter: 'A' and 'B' (upper) for those forward of the bridge, 'X' and 'Y' (lower) for those mounted aft.

Above: To illustrate the range of *Belfast*'s main armament, the guns of 'A' and 'B' turrets have been trained and elevated on to a target 12½ miles away in the northwest of London, the London Gateway motorway services area on the M1. Whilst this sounds impressive, she was actually capable of hitting enemy targets at a maximum range of approximately 14 miles and each gun could fire up to eight rounds per minute. The middle gun is mounted 2ft 6in abaft of the wing guns to reduce interference between the shells in flight. This arrangement also improved the turret's balance and increased the space between the gun crews.

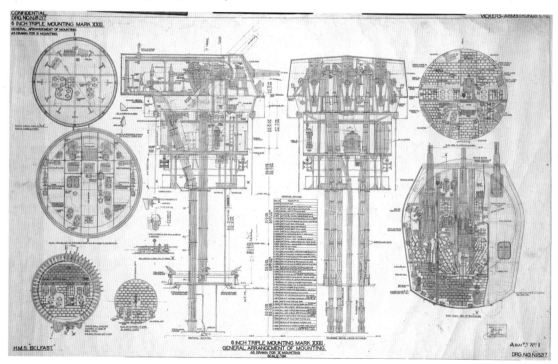

Above: Prepared by Vickers Armstrong Ltd, these 1938 drawings illustrate the layout of each 6in mounting including the turret, hoists, shell room and magazine handling room. The Mk XXIII mounting differed from its immediate predecessor in having longer hoists for the shells and cordite charges; one result of this was the placing of the two after turrets one deck higher than in earlier ships of the Town class. (© *National Maritime Museum, Greenwich, London*)

Right: The port side 6in gun within 'A' turret. The recoil cylinder can be clearly seen immediately below the closed breech block.

Below: The officer of turret's position which includes the turret bearing indicator, telephone and voice pipes to the local sight cabinet, working chamber and shell room.

Bottom: The hand-operated breech block of 'A' turret's port side gun in the open position. Each gun could be independently elevated between 5° depression and 45° either by power or hand. The blue wheel in the background could be used by the layer, whose nearby seat can also be seen, to manually control the elevation of the gun.

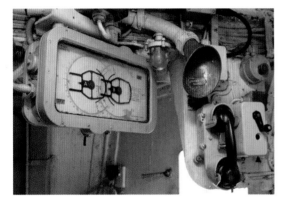

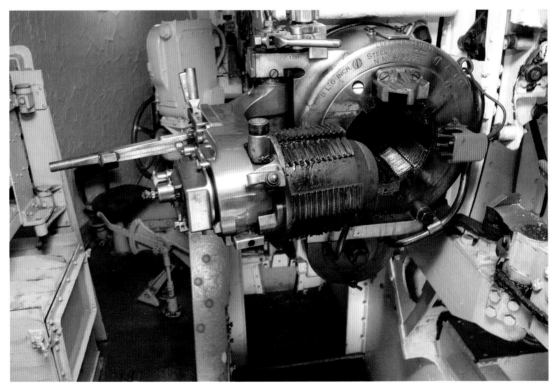

Above: 'A' turret's interior showing the cramped working conditions that were endured by the gun crews who would have been closed up inside for hours on end. Sadly, barriers are now a necessity to keep visitors away from the potentially dangerous equipment on the other side.

Top right: On arrival in the turret, each shell was pushed out of the tilting bucket, at the top of the shell hoist, into this intermediate tray which can be moved up and down on curved rails.

Bottom left: When the intermediate tray and gun loading tray were moved into line, the shell dropped into the gun loading tray. As the breech opened, the loading tray would be swung forward into line with the bore, the shell rammed home, followed by the cordite charge and the closure of the breech. Having carefully studied the interior of 'A' turret it is well worth visiting the 'Gun Turret Experience: A Sailor's Story, 1943' which brings 'Y' turret back to life with lights, sound, smoke effects, videos and projections. This exciting exhibition was developed by the IWM in 2011 to provide *Belfast's* visitors with a better impression of the hectic and cramped conditions experienced by the twenty-seven men who worked inside each 6in turret.

Bottom right: Each 30lb cordite charge was stored in an anti-flash cardboard container until it could be loaded into the gun. It consisted of cordite sticks tied together with silk thread and sewn into a silk bag. The charge is seen following its arrival in the gun turret via the pedal-operated hand-up scuttle. The doors at either end of this metal tube are interlocked to prevent both being opened at the same time. A maximum of eight cordite rounds per minute could be supplied to the gun turret via the scuttle.

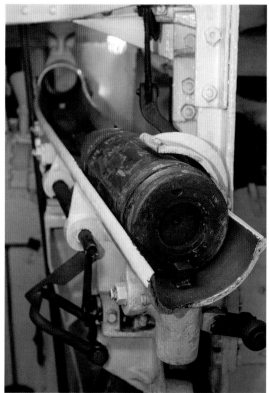

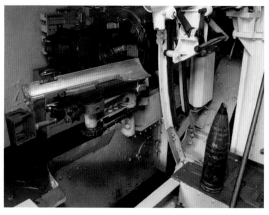

THE SHELL ROOMS

Separate shell rooms, with a crew of nine men, served each 6in gun turret. Located below the waterline, they are the most heavily protected compartments, along with the cordite handling rooms and magazines, due to the combination of the 4½in main armour belt and the 3in armoured deck situated immediately above the shell rooms.

If an explosion appeared to be imminent, the magazines and shell rooms could have been swiftly flooded by opening the seacock, via the rod gearing within the flooding locker on the weather deck or by the magazine escape, to allow water in through the 7in flood pipe. However, the crews would have had virtually no chance of escape.

Right: Two 6in shells sitting in the loading bays at the bottom of the electrically-driven duplex endless chain hoists that run between 'B' turret and its shell room. Each hoist could deliver a maximum of ten rounds per minute to the turret.

Below: The powered revolving shell ring could hold a total of fifty-six 6in shells.

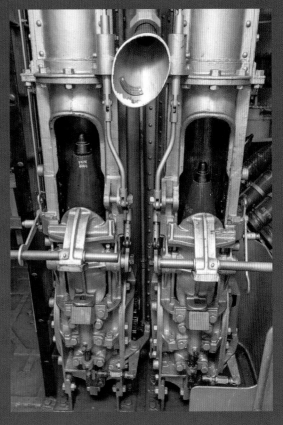

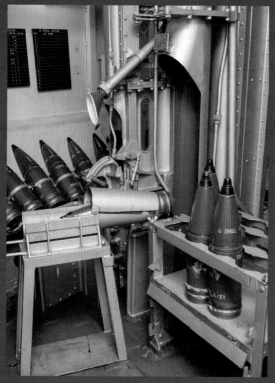

Left: Each 112lb shell was moved by hand from the revolving shell ring and loaded into the next available holder at the bottom of the shell hoist for the journey up to the gun turret.

Below left: The 6in shells were stored in the wooden bins in the foreground. When required, the shells were moved by hand from the bins to the revolving shell ring prior to loading in one of the shell hoists. In 1948 the ship had stowage for a total of 2,862 shells, mostly CPC and high explosive, together with some rounds for practice and drill purposes.

Below right: The metal casings which contain the separate shell and cordite hoists can be clearly seen in this view of the void between 'B' turret's shell room and the underside of the access platform.

Opposite: 6in shells lie base first in the revolving shell ring. This could move independently of the turret above. Shells were painted different colours according to type; this colour coding was a practice which had come into use during the middle of the nineteenth century as more and more types of ammunition entered service and the need for quick identification in action became evident.

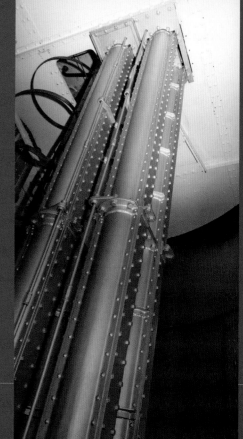

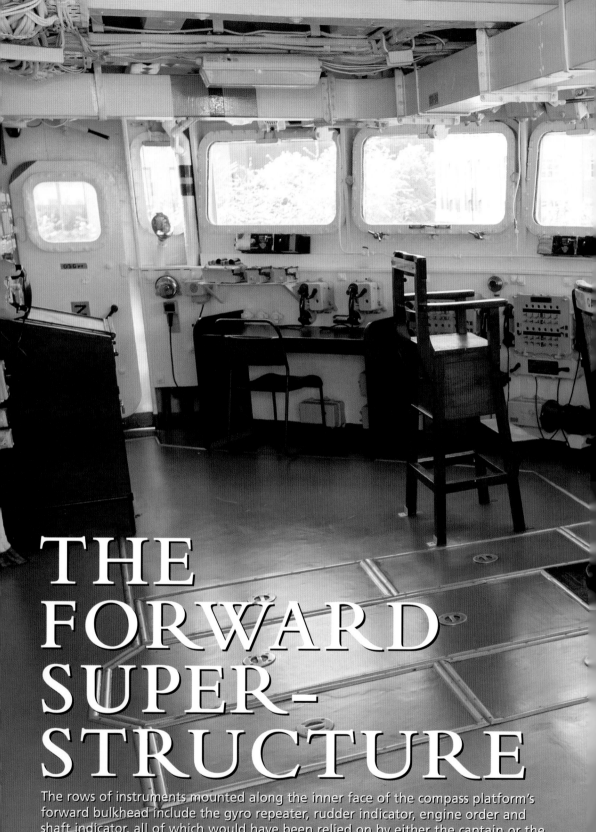

THE FORWARD SUPER-STRUCTURE

The rows of instruments mounted along the inner face of the compass platform's forward bulkhead include the gyro repeater, rudder indicator, engine order and shaft indicator, all of which would have been relied on by either the captain or the officer of the watch while handling the ship.

THE PRESENT FORWARD SUPERSTRUCTURE IS THE most distinctive external feature to have been fitted during *Belfast*'s 1956–59 modernisation. The provision of a large, fully enclosed compass platform and an admiral's bridge provided a significant improvement in the working conditions of those who manned these areas. The main 6in director was the only major external piece of equipment to be retained (and even this was updated); the open compass platform with its distinctive curved front and wind baffles, the former aircraft hangars (converted to crew space in 1944–45), the light AA guns and the tripod foremast were all replaced.

Above: The external pipework fitted to the forward superstructure contained a series of nozzles as part of the ship's pre-wetting system, which was designed to reduce the effect of nuclear fallout by washing away radioactive material from the external surfaces. The system would have been turned on if warning was received of an imminent attack and used sea water from the ship's salt water system.

Below: This smart row of opening scuttles along the port side of the forward superstructure on 1 deck provided natural light and ventilation to the heads that were reserved for the exclusive use of chief petty officers and petty officers.

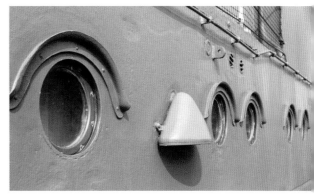

Above: With its imposing five-sided tiered facade, the forward superstructure is sometimes described as the ship's nerve centre due to the combination of the compass platform, operations room, gun direction platform, admiral's bridge, bridge wireless office and flag deck within its metalwork. On 02 deck, the single MRS8 controlled-range blind fire director, together with two 40mm Bofors twin RP 50 Mark 5 mountings, mounted either side of the forward superstructure, formed two-thirds of the ship's close-range anti-aircraft armament.

Left: The forward end of the mounting bracket for the medium frequency direction-finder provided the perfect prominent position on which to mount a large version of the ship's official badge (see p.88) made from aluminium alloy.

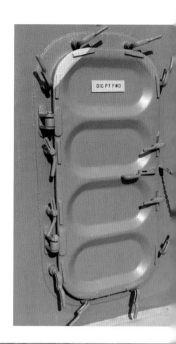

Opposite, far left: The port side navigation light mounted above the admiral's bridge.

Opposite, top middle: The aerial frame for the medium frequency direction-finder.

Opposite, top right: The single action airtight and watertight door mounted in the leading edge of the forward superstructure on 01 deck.

Opposite, bottom left: In this view of the foremast's port side, the Type 277Q height-finding radar can be clearly seen on the lowest platform, with a daylight signalling lantern in between the radar and the mast itself. On the platform above is the semi-circular Type 978 navigation radar, while the wind direction transmitter extends forward of the mast's top platform.

Opposite, bottom right: One of the port 40mm Bofors.

Right: The front elevation of the foremast. The two light-signalling lanterns can be seen either side of the Type 277Q radar and Type AJE aerials are visible at the end of the upper yardarms. The semi-circular Type 293Q high-definition surface warning radar tops the main section of the foremast.

Below: This one-ton electric winch is one of a pair that is mounted on 01 deck immediately ahead of the forward superstructure.

Bottom left: The 'pigeonholes' inside the signal flag locker in the flag deck's aft port quarter.

Bottom right: The 20in and 10in (in the foreground) signal projectors on the port side of the flag deck enabled the signal men to maintain radio silence while communicating with other ships in visual range.

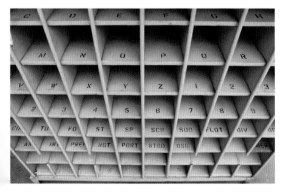

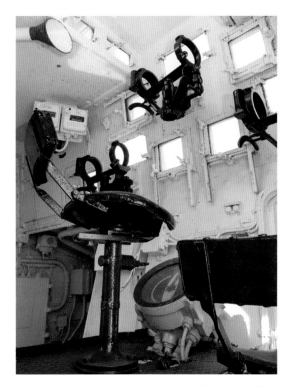

Above: Six men would have worked within the cramped aft section of the forward director control tower (DCT) for the 6in main armament. The DCT could be trained at a rate of up to 180° in twenty seconds, or just half a degree in one minute.

Above: Rear view of the DCT. It determined the target's range and bearing, which was fed to the 6in transmitting station to be converted into the required angles of elevation and training for the 6in guns.

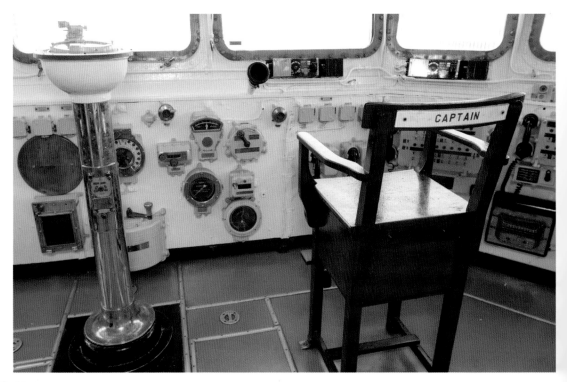

Right: The semi-enclosed charthouse is located in the compass platform's aft starboard quarter. In addition to the large chart table, where the navigating officer and his assistants plotted the ship's course, the compartment contained all of the charts and pilots that were likely to be required during the ship's deployment.

Opposite, bottom: The inner face of the compass platform's forward bulkhead. In between the pelorus and the captain's chair can be seen a cluster of five instruments – clockwise from the bottom: the starboard shafts' speed and direction, the ship's speed, the distance run, the rudder position indicator, and the revolution order receiver.

Left and bottom left: The dramatic increase in the amount of electrical equipment fitted during the modernisation is underlined by the proliferation of cabling and junction boxes mounted to the compass platform's aft bulkhead.

Bottom middle: The steering order transmitter. Whenever the captain or the officer of the watch required a change in the rudder's position, he could pass on his instructions to the helmsman, standing six decks below in the forward steering position, by turning the wheel in the middle of the steering order transmitter. Contact could also be maintained between the forward steering position and the compass platform using either the intercom or voice pipe.

Bottom right: To ensure that the navigating officer could be present whenever required, his cabin was situated opposite the charthouse. Despite his senior position within the ship's company, this cabin was quite spartan, although it had the relative luxury of a fixed scuttle and stainless steel sink.

OPERATIONS ROOM

UNTIL 2010 THE OPERATIONS ROOM WAS SET up to portray the scene during the Battle of North Cape. Although the mannequins wore uniforms of the right era, they were in fact surrounded by equipment from the late 1950s. This discrepancy was dealt with during the 2010–2011 restoration. The results are part of the IWM's current policy to reduce the number of barriers and allow members of the public up close to the exhibits as well as bringing them back to life whenever possible. In the case of *Belfast*'s operations room this meant using a combination of animated rotating radar screens, authentic sound effects and interactive games. The new theme follows the events of a major exercise during *Belfast*'s final deployment to the Far East in April 1961. Code named Pony Express, it involved sixty warships, 20,000 naval personnel and 6,000 troops off North Borneo in the South China Sea. Visitors are invited to control the movements of the ships which in turn activates a range of visual and audio effects.

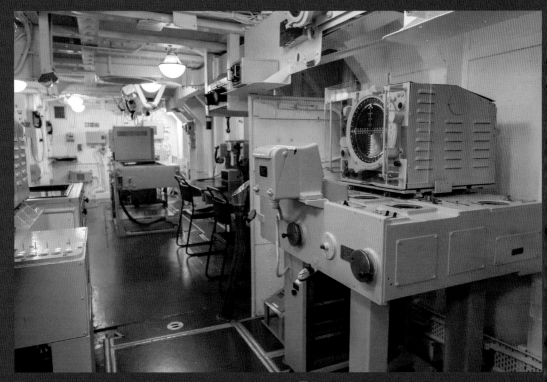

Above left: The air plotting area, situated along the port side, portrayed the position of friendly and enemy aircraft. It also provided the means to co-ordinate the activities of allied strike and fighter aircraft operating in the area. As forces rehearsed a full-scale amphibious landing on the island of Balam Bangan during Pony Express, one of the Scimitar ground attack aircraft from HMS *Victorious* ditched offshore. The ensuing salvage operation forms the basis for the interactive games that have been sympathetically incorporated within two of the plotting tables.

Left: The radar display in the foreground forms part of the gun direction area while the tables in the background are within the surface plotting area.

Above: Using the information displayed from the radar, the officers and ratings of the gun direction area, located in the heart of the operations room, selected the targets to be engaged with the ship's armament.

Bottom right: Located along the starboard side, at the forward end of the operations room, the surface plotting area contained these plotting tables on which the local surface and underwater situations were depicted.

Above: *Belfast* regularly served as a flagship throughout her time in commission. A separate bridge enabled the admiral to exercise tactical command of a fleet or squadron without hindering the work of the ship's officers on the compass platform.

Middle left: The gyro repeater on the admiral's bridge.

Below left: By flicking one of these switches, the admiral or his staff could use the intercom to communicate with the ship's senior officers.

Bottom right: Two 'stateboards' on the admiral's bridge enabled the embarked flag officer and his staff to keep track of the overall tactical situation.

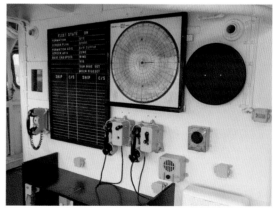

Above: The VHF/UHF equipment room, situated on 1 deck of the forward superstructure, contained the VHF and UHF transmitting and receiving equipment and associated power amplifiers. This equipment could be tuned to the designated frequencies and input or output then 'piped' to the required section of the ship, including the bridge wireless office (BWO) on 02 deck of the forward superstructure, which acted as the ship's communications centre.

Bottom left: Detail of a transmitter power amplifier unit in the VHF/UHF equipment room. The numbered black dials were to tune the amplifier for maximum power output by watching for the peak reading on the meter, at which point the dials would be locked in place using the little silver coloured levers.

Bottom right: Sea cabins for the admiral and the captain are located aft of the admiral's bridge on 02 deck. Smaller sea cabins, like this one, are located on the deck below and were reserved for less senior officers.

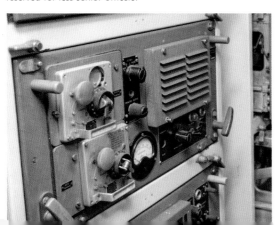

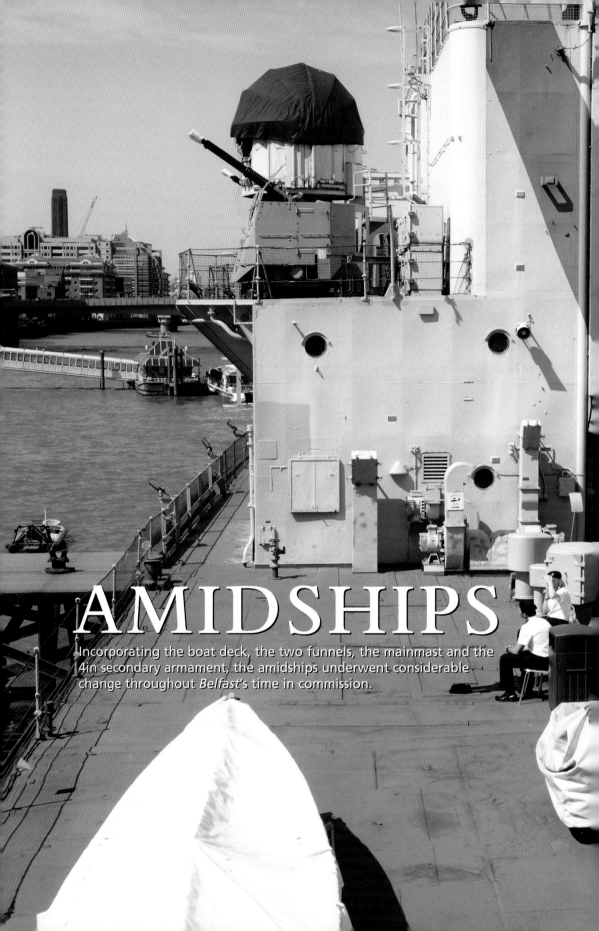

AMIDSHIPS

Incorporating the boat deck, the two funnels, the mainmast and the 4in secondary armament, the amidships underwent considerable change throughout *Belfast*'s time in commission.

Below: Looking forward along the port side from the top of the deck house that replaced the aft twin 4in mounting. To compensate for the increased top weight of the additional close range anti-aircraft armament fitted during *Belfast*'s 1944–45 refit, it was decided to remove the aft pair of 4in mountings. The remaining four mountings continued to form part of *Belfast*'s armament for the rest of her naval service and were fired in anger for the last time during the Korean War.

Above and below right: *Belfast* was originally fitted with twelve high angle/low angle, quick-firing, Mark XVI, all steel construction, 4in guns, dispersed between six twin Mark XIX mountings fitted with an extended shield made of ⅛in protective plating. The guns could be used against surface targets in addition to their primary anti-aircraft role. Each mounting weighs 15.5 tons and the individual guns could fire a maximum of between fifteen and twenty rounds per minute at targets up to 21,300 yards away (approximately 12 miles).

Below left: Once the 4in shells had been brought up from the magazines, they were moved aft along the deck by a Simplex chain conveyor and stowed in ready-use lockers in between the mountings.

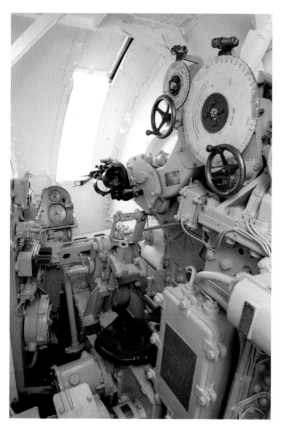

The forward 4in mounting, on the starboard side, is seen in August 2012 towards the end of a two and a half year long restoration by a group of dedicated volunteers.

Left: A close-up view of the elevating position on the left-hand side of the mounting. By using the handles, the guns could be elevated to any angle from 10° depression to 80°. Each revolution of the handles elevated the gun by another 3°.

Below: The two 4in guns are of the quick-firing type, with breech blocks that move downwards to open, thereby allowing them to be mounted more closely in a common cradle which elevates both guns together. Each gun is equipped with its own recoil and run-out arrangement. The elevating and training positions can be clearly seen on the front left- and right-hand sides of the mounting respectively. The fuse setting trays were retained on the left- and right-hand side at the back of the mounting, following the removal of the fuse setting machine, to provide a rest position for the ammunition.

Opposite: When required, the 35lb shells were moved by hand from their metal tube within the 4in magazine and loaded into one of the flash tight duplex chain hoists that brought them up on deck for transfer via the Simplex conveyor to either the ready-use locker or direct to the waiting gun crew on the mounting.

Below left: Stowed in rows of open-ended metal tubes, up to four hundred starshell and two thousand high-explosive shells could be stowed within the 4in magazine on 5 deck.

Below right: A metal retaining clip ensured that each shell remained within its tube until it was needed.

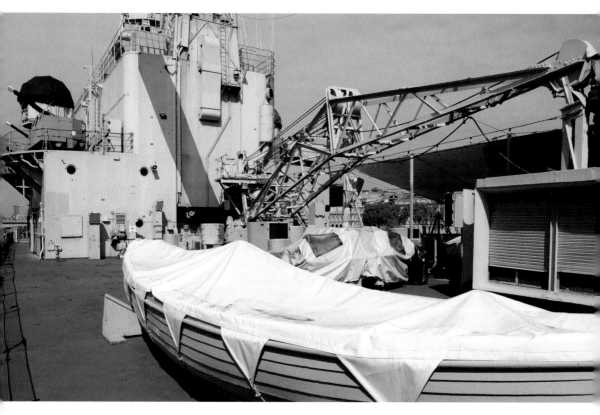

Above: In 1939 this deck was fitted with an athwartships fixed cordite Type D1H catapult, which extended to a length of 92ft, to launch the two embarked Supermarine Walrus amphibians at a speed of 55.5 knots. Nicknamed 'shagbat', these remarkably resilient aircraft primarily acted as the 'eyes of the fleet' in the spotter reconnaissance role and were accommodated within the forward superstructure's two hangars. The aircraft were moved on a trolley that ran on rails from the hangar to the catapult turntable. At the end of its mission, the Walrus would be brought back on board by one of the 7-ton electric cranes mounted either side of the fore funnel. The advent of more powerful radar combined with increasing numbers of aircraft carriers and the need to reutilise valuable deck space resulted in the landing of *Belfast*'s aircraft in June 1943. During the 1944–45 refit, the catapult was removed, along with one of the cranes, and the hangars were converted into additional accommodation, while the sole remaining crane was moved to its current position to handle the craft that were to be stowed on the new boat deck. By day, the boat deck is now a delightful place for visitors to enjoy a leisurely drink or snack from the appropriately named Walrus Café which is located within the space once occupied by the port side hangar. When the ship closes to the public for the night, it is used during the summer months for private receptions organised by Sodexo Prestige.

Right: Detail of *Belfast*'s sole remaining 7-ton electric seaplane crane.

Above: FMD5385 is one of the last 16ft Fast Motor Dinghies which were more commonly known throughout the Fleet as the 'skimmer', or 'skimming dish'. FMD5385 was built by John Bushell Ltd of Wargrave as part of the order for eight new FMDs placed in October 1953. Powered by a Coventry Climax supercharged 2-stroke diesel engine to a top speed of 21 knots, the FMDs were allocated to destroyers, sloops and any warship that carried aircraft, including *Belfast* which embarked one during WWII. They were generally used to ferry up to seven men ashore and reserved for the captain's personal use in destroyers. In calm conditions they were fun to drive but proved to be very 'wet' in a choppy sea.

FMD5385 endured a chequered career following her sale by the Navy. She eventually sank in Dartmouth Harbour and was rescued by Lt Col A K Stephenson, DFC, who set up the Dartmouth Skimming Dish Restoration Group which restored FMD5385 to her former glory and presented her to the IWM for display onboard *Belfast* on 9 January 1991.

16ft Fast Motor Dinghy Specification

Length Overall	16ft
Length Water-line	15ft
Beam	5ft 6in
Draught	1ft 5in
Displacement	0.9 ton
Designer	John Samuel White & Co Ltd

Right, upper: The wooden clinker 27ft whaler which is similar to the whalers carried by *Belfast* on gantries below the flight deck until 1940. A pair of 27ft whalers was subsequently re-embarked in 1945. Following the modernisation *Belfast* carried four whalers: two motorised versions, held in davits, and a pair of sailing/pulling whalers, stowed in cradles on the boat deck

Right, lower: Some of the mushroom top vents on the boat deck which could be closed up if required.

Above and above right: Topped by a Type 960M long-range air warning radar, the tubular lattice mast replaced the original tripod mast during the 1956–59 modernisation. A routine inspection in 2007 revealed that the ship's two lattice masts were suffering from severe corrosion that was destroying the metalwork from the inside out. This presented *Belfast's* conservation team with a difficult dilemma. On the one hand, they are charged with preserving as much of the ship's original fabric as possible, yet ensuring the public's safety remains paramount at all times. Further investigation confirmed that it would have been virtually impossible to safely repair the original masts. Thus, the IWM gratefully accepted an offer from a group of Russian companies to pay for the fabrication of two new masts by a team of twenty men and women from the JSC Shipbuilding plant, Severnaya Verf in St Petersburg.

The work took eighteen months to complete and culminated in some of the Russian shipbuilders flying to London in September 2010 to spend six weeks dismantling the old masts and installing the new ones as a lasting tribute to those involved in the Arctic convoys of WWII. The completion of this work was marked by the unveiling of a permanent memorial (p.90) on the quarterdeck on 19 October 2010 in the presence of HRH The Duke of Edinburgh and veterans of the Arctic convoys.

Below right: Following the modernisation, each 4in turret could be operated in conjunction with its own dedicated MRS8 Controlled Range Blind Fire Director. The director for the aft port side 4in turret can be seen in between the aft funnel and mainmast.

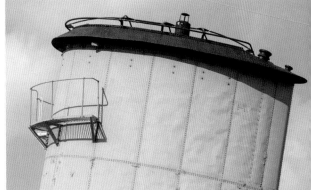

Above, top right and middle right: The raked funnels were a distinctive feature of *Belfast*'s appearance. Their position aft of the boat deck ensured that the smoke was kept clear of the forward superstructure. Fortunately, their proposed replacement with upright funnels similar to those on later cruisers was dropped from the schedule of work for the 1956–59 modernisation.

Bottom right: The air intakes for the forward boiler room are located immediately ahead of the forward funnel. The roller shutters would have been closed to smarten up the appearance of the ship whenever *Belfast* was alongside and the boilers were not in use.

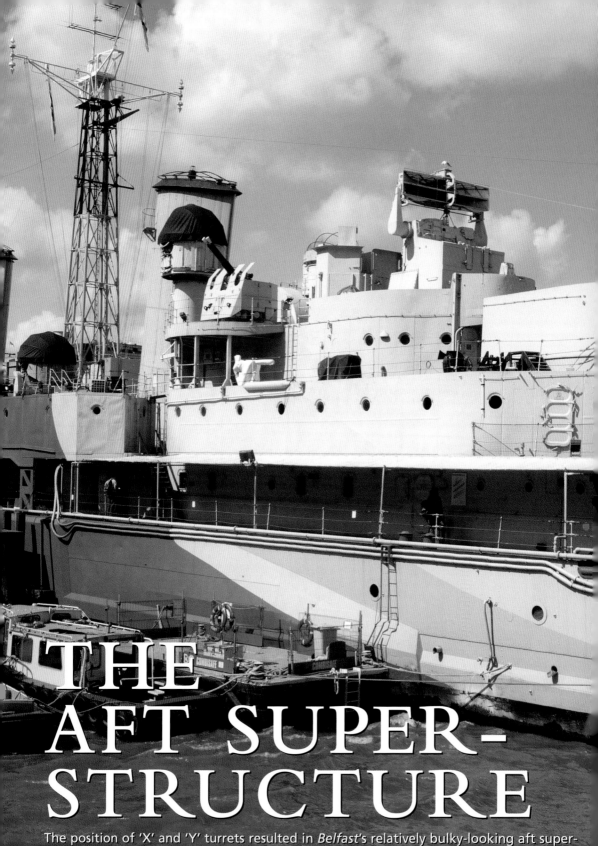

THE AFT SUPER- STRUCTURE

The position of 'X' and 'Y' turrets resulted in *Belfast*'s relatively bulky-looking aft super-structure. However, her improved level of stability after the fitting of bulges enabled *Belfast* to retain 'X' turret despite the additional top weight gained by upgrading her anti-aircraft armament during WWII.

Above left: During *Belfast*'s 1956–59 modernisation, all of her existing close-range anti-aircraft armament was removed and replaced by six 40mm Bofors twin RP 50 Mark 5 mountings. Four were fitted two on either side of the forward superstructure and the remaining pair were fitted ahead of the emergency conning position on the aft superstructure. Weighing 6 tons, each mounting is fitted with a ½in protective plate at the front and ¼in protective plates at the sides. The Mark 11 water-cooled Bofors guns could be fired individually or as a pair, and elevated to any angle from 14° depression to 90° while the mounting could be trained through a full 360°. The high-explosive 40mm shells, fitted with direct action fuses, could be fired at a rate of 120 rounds per minute when the guns were elevated at 60°, while a rate of 140 rounds per minute was possible when the guns were at 0° elevation.

Above and opposite, bottom: When used in conjunction with the Type 262 radar of the adjacent blind fire director, the 40mm Bofors could be automatically operated by day or night against targets up to a maximum range of 2,500 yards. The mounting is fitted with the all-electric RP 50 metadyne system which enabled the blind fire director to automatically control the elevation and training of the guns. The guns could be fired electronically via the blind fire director or the joystick, mounted on the left-hand side of the mounting, which also controlled the elevation and training of the guns in the latter mode. In the event of a power failure, the guns could be fired mechanically by using the layer's foot-operated pedal. In these circumstances, the training and elevation was achieved by using the handles fitted either side of the guns.

Left: Detail of the elevation receiver.

Right and below: A total of eight MRS8 controlled range blind fire directors were fitted during *Belfast's* 1956–59 modernisation. Four were added amidships to work in conjunction with each 4in mounting, one was fitted either side of the forward superstructure to control the 40mm Bofors guns, while the remaining pair were installed on the aft superstructure to be used with the other pair of 40mm Bofors guns. Each blind fire director is fitted with Type 262 radar which proved ideally suited for the 40mm Bofors and inadequate for the longer range of the 4in guns. In home waters, the blind fire directors were topped with black canvas covers, which were exchanged for white ones during her service in the Far East in a bid to slightly lower the extreme temperatures that built up within the directors while operating in the region.

Left: *Belfast* would have been commanded from this emergency conning position in the event of the compass platform being knocked out of action. The lower section of this structure housed the ready-use magazine for the two 40mm Bofors mountings.

Above: A close-up view of the rear of the aft 6in director control tower's Type 274 fire control radar, fitted during her 1944–45 refit, and retained after her 1956–59 modernisation.

Right: This wooden board recorded the whereabouts of the ship's senior officers whenever she was alongside, anchored or moored to a buoy.

Below and bottom: Even though the majority of the ship is open to the public, it was decided to reserve a small number of compartments for the hosting of private functions to provide an additional source of income towards *Belfast*'s long-term preservation. Today these events are organised by the company Sodexo Prestige which caters annually for approximately 18,000 people across 375 events including summer deck parties, conferences, private dinners and even weddings – *Belfast* was officially licensed as a wedding venue in 2007. The wardroom anteroom, used by the officers for pre-dinner drinks and general relaxation, has been meticulously restored to its 1959 appearance. Today, it is used for dinners, conferences and other functions for up to fifty people. *(Lower image courtesy Sodexo Prestige)*

Above and left: Located below the quarterdeck, on 3 deck, these cabins would have been occupied by the admiral in harbour. The admiral's dining room has been restored to its 1959 appearance. Today, the admiral's dining room is capable of accommodating up to eighteen people for either private dinners or meetings. During *Belfast*'s time in commission, the food would have been prepared in the pantry which is located immediately ahead of this compartment on the port side. At the appropriate moment, the food would have been passed through a small set of double doors, above the sideboard on the right hand side of this image, and served by the admiral's stewards. The admiral's day cabin can be seen through the open doorway. *(Both images courtesy of Sodexo Prestige)*

Bottom left: The admiral's day cabin is one of the few cabins onboard to have curtains that could be drawn across the scuttles.

Opposite, top: The admiral's day cabin is now used for pre-dinner drinks by those who hire the adjacent admiral's dining room. Originally, this would have been used by the admiral for relaxation and hosting informal meetings. The large picture frame, on the left-hand side of the image, contains the medals and orders awarded to Admiral Sir Robert Burnett, GBE, KCB, DSO, LLD, who flew his flag in *Belfast* during the Battle of North Cape.

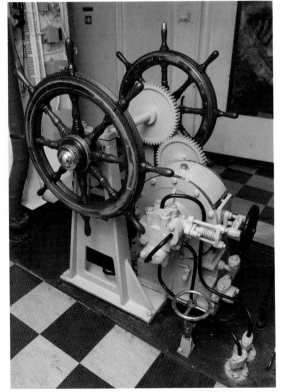

Left: The emergency steering position is situated on 3 deck, immediately ahead of the hatch that leads down to the tiller flat. The bracket holding the nearest wooden wheel is in fact a modern replica to replace the original bracket which was removed at some point before *Belfast*'s arrival in the Thames. It seemed a strange item to remove, because in contrast to some of the other missing equipment, such as the 40mm Bofors mountings, it would not have had any use on another warship.

Above: The emergency steering position's compass and rudder indicator.

THE TILLER FLAT

Left: Situated immediately above the single 207sq ft balanced rudder, the tiller flat contains an electro-hydraulic four ram unit. One of the two 60bhp electric motors that provided the power for the hydraulic system can be seen in the left foreground, connected to a hydraulic pump, located within the green casing. An identical arrangement is present within the forward steering gear compartment which is located immediately ahead of the tiller flat. The forward (primary) and secondary steering positions operated transmitter rams which relayed the wheel's movements by pumping hydraulic fluid to and from the telemotor receivers in the steering gear compartment. These signals were in turn transmitted via mechanical links and levers to the four hydraulic rams which worked directly on to the rudder crosshead. The telemotor system proved to be more reliable in action compared to electrical systems. Damage or flooding usually resulted in the failure of the electrical system due to broken wires, whereas the telemotor system pipes tended to stretch and bend rather than break.

Below: The four hydraulic rams that directly worked on to the rudder crosshead occupy the bulk of the tiller flat.

Far left: In the event that the forward steering position became inoperable or both telemotor systems failed, the ship would have to be steered from the secondary steering position, located behind the watertight door on the left-hand side of the image, in the tiller flat.

Left: The hydraulic pressures within the four cylinders that hold the rams could be monitored via these gauges. The mechanical links and levers which operated the four rams can be seen in the foreground

Right: Counter-weights connected to wires and pulleys enable one person to open the 2in armoured hatch which weighs 650lb and leads down to the tiller flat.

THE QUARTERDECK

Right: Adorned with two copies of the ship's official badge, this is one of two lifebelts mounted on the after screen which flank *Belfast*'s bell. As the first of the Royal Navy's warships to be named *Belfast*, an official badge had to be specifically designed for her. By chance, whilst considering various ideas for the badge's design, the ship's first senior engineer, Lt Stuart Ferguson, started thinking about the seahorse skeleton he had picked up during a walk along the shores of Lake Avernus in southern Italy. Since the coat of arms for the City of Belfast also contains two seahorses it seemed entirely appropriate that a seahorse should form the basis of the ship's badge, so Lt Ferguson submitted a set of drawings to the Admiralty that were passed to the College of Arms to be turned into the ship's official badge. The final result is topped by a naval crown, with the ship's motto, *Pro tanto quid retribuamus*, reproduced underneath. Shared with the namesake city, this means, 'What shall we give in return for so much?' However, the ship's company devised their own interpretation, 'We give as good as we get.' Stuart Ferguson subsequently donated the skeleton which inspired the design of the ship's badge to the HMS *Belfast* Trust.

Unofficial badges were increasingly used by the Royal Navy's warships from the mid nineteenth century onwards. In December 1918 the Admiralty established the Ships' Badges Committee to oversee the allocation of suitable official badges to every warship. Before 1976, the shape of a ship's badge varied according to the type of warship. Cruisers were allocated badges with a pentagonal ground.

Below: The wooden battle honours board and the silver bell are mounted to the after screen which is situated immediately beneath 'Y' turret. The partially glazed, split opening, wooden door leads to the quartermaster's lobby.

Right: The strength of the bond between the City of Belfast and the cruiser is clearly represented by this magnificent silver bell. It was paid for by public subscription during the ship's construction and intended as an elaborate ornament that would pass to all future warships of the same name. However, the official presentation was postponed due to the outbreak of WWII and did not take place until the ship returned to Belfast in October 1948. It remained on board until November 1962 when it was returned to the Lord Mayor of Belfast to await the commissioning of a future HMS *Belfast*. However, the combination of the cruiser's preservation and the absence of a successor in the Royal Navy led to its presentation, for a second time, to the ship by the Lord Mayor of Belfast on 21 October 1977. The engraving along the shoulder and the sound ring record the background to the commissioning of the bell, while an elaborate reproduction of the city's coat of arms dominates the bell's waist.

Like all warships, *Belfast* was also issued with a standard ship's bell by the Admiralty. This bell is now on public display at the Ulster Folk & Transport Museum which is located just a few miles away from where *Belfast* was built at the Harland & Wolff shipyard.

Below right: In keeping with naval tradition, the names of all the children who were born to serving members of the ship's company and baptised using the upturned ship's bell as a font have been engraved along the inner surface of the sound ring.

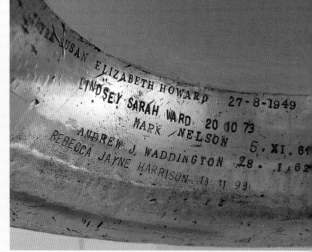

Above: Initially located on the quarterdeck, this plaque has been moved to the boat deck and marks the successful completion of the project to replace the lattice masts as a tribute to those involved in the Arctic convoys of WWII.

Right: The quarterdeck is the last of the ship's external decks to be clad in wooden planking. The majority of *Belfast*'s external decks were originally clad with Borneo white hard wooden planking. However, they were all removed, with the exception of the quarterdeck, during *Belfast*'s 1956–59 modernisation. At the invitation of the IWM, the Worshipful Company of Shipwrights arranged for the quarterdeck to be replanked in 1986 by apprentices supervised by Colin Parker.

Above: The tread plate by the top of the aft starboard accommodation ladder.

Far left: The battle honour boards displayed by many of the Royal Navy's warships record the conflicts in which ships of the same name have participated since the defeat of the Spanish Armada in 1588. For many years warships carried elaborate scrolls, on an unofficial basis, commemorating the significant events that ships of the same name had been involved in. These lists were usually the result of research by a member of the ship's company and sometimes included events that were not subsequently recognised as official battle honours. The Royal Navy finally introduced a formal system to regulate the approval and use of battle honours on 1 October 1954 via Admiralty Fleet Order 2565. Its primary objectives were to foster an esprit de corps and encourage a greater interest in naval history. Generally, a battle honour is awarded for those actions resulting in the defeat of the enemy, or when the action was inconclusive but well fought and in exceptional cases where outstanding efforts were made against overwhelming odds. A battle honour is not awarded for a British defeat or when the action was inconclusive and badly fought. Today, the Royal Navy's warships can only display those battle honours which are officially approved by the Ministry of Defence.

In the case of HMS *Belfast*, she is the Royal Navy's only warship to bear the name and therefore earned the four battle honours that are proudly displayed on this wooden board mounted by the quartermaster's lobby.

Left: Whenever the 6in guns were not required for use they were fitted with watertight plugs, known as tompions, which carried a medallion in the form of the ship's badge.

Right: The aft capstan was used primarily to handle the stern lines while berthing.

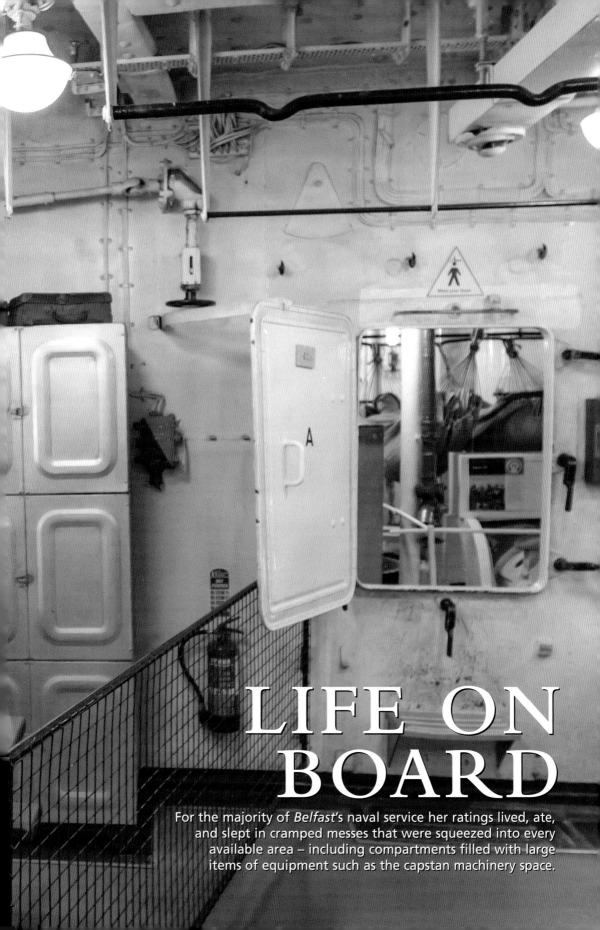

LIFE ON
BOARD

For the majority of *Belfast*'s naval service her ratings lived, ate,
and slept in cramped messes that were squeezed into every
available area – including compartments filled with large
items of equipment such as the capstan machinery space.

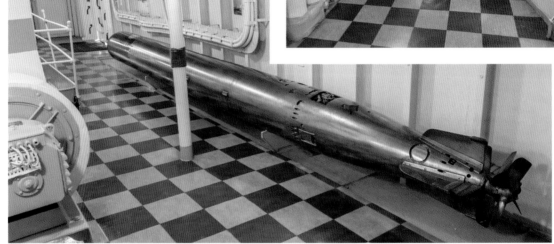

IMPROVING THE LIVING CONDITIONS OF
Belfast's ship's company was a major factor during the planning of her 1956–59 modernisation. To achieve this objective, surplus bulky items of equipment, such as the two sets of triple torpedo tubes, were removed to free up valuable space that could be reutilised for other purposes.

Top right and above: The torpedo flat is so-called because the starboard set of revolving triple torpedo tubes were located in this position until *Belfast*'s 1956–59 modernisation when the mounting was removed and its open firing ports were plated over. *Belfast* only carried the six 21in Mark IX torpedoes that could be physically accommodated within both sets of triple tubes. A torpedo control sight was fitted to each side of the upper bridge. During the final stages of *Scharnhorst*'s destruction, fifty-five torpedoes were fired at the stricken battlecruiser, including three from *Belfast*'s starboard tubes.

Top left: The range setting equipment for the 21in Mark IX torpedo.

Left: The exterior of the uptake and down take spaces running between the forward boiler room and the forward funnel can be seen along the right-hand side of this image.

Above: These washing machines could take 100lb of washing at a time and were operated around the clock along with the tumble driers to clean clothing for the ship's company. The removal of the torpedo armament during *Belfast*'s modernisation enabled the former torpedo parting shop, where the torpedoes were armed and disarmed, to be converted into a modern well-equipped ship's laundry. Previously, the ratings had washed their clothes in whatever came to hand, including bathrooms, basins and buckets. Whenever *Belfast* was assigned to the Far East Fleet, her ship's company included an influx of two types of Chinese men from Hong Kong. The 'official Chinese' consisted of uniformed ratings serving as cooks and stewards on detachment from HMS *Tamar* in Hong Kong, while 'unofficial Chinese' were authorised tradesmen who were allowed to work, on a commercial basis, as laundrymen, tailors or shoemakers and live in the ship. Thus *Belfast*'s laundry was operated by a team of ten 'unofficial Chinese' laundrymen during her time in the Far East Fleet. At all other times, specially trained ratings operated the service on behalf of the ship's company.

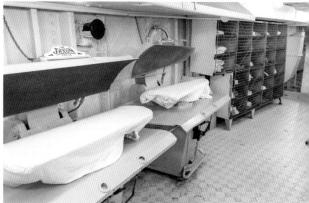

Right: The pressing equipment within *Belfast*'s laundry.

Above: The shipwright's workshop.

Below: Letters and parcels provided the only direct link between those serving in the ship and the families they had left behind at home. Therefore the efficient dispatch and arrival of the post via the mail room could play an important part in boosting the morale of the ship's company during their long overseas tours.

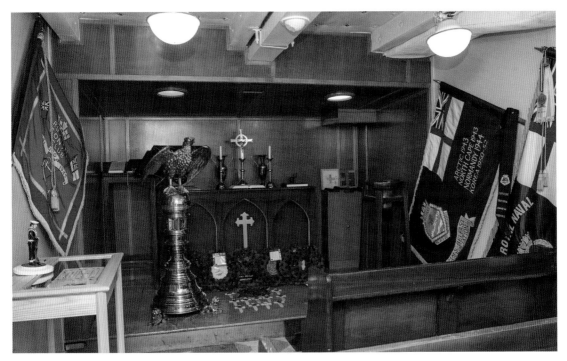

Above: Despite its small size, the chapel played an important role in the daily lives of the ship's company, especially during her active wartime service. The majority of the altar furniture on display comes from other decommissioned warships, although a few items, such as the lectern, have been donated by churches and private individuals as personal acts of remembrance. The chapel, home to the official standards of the HMS *Belfast* Association, the Russian Convoy Club and the Battersea branch of the Royal Naval Association when they are not required for ceremonial events, is still occasionally used for christenings and private services.

Below: Following *Belfast*'s modernisation, the ship's company could relax and listen to the latest music and radio programmes via speakers connected to the sound reproduction equipment room.

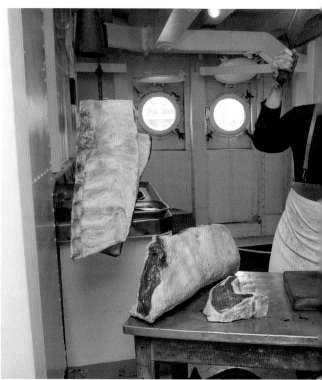

Top left: The door to the refrigerated galley ready-use store.

Top middle: In the course of eighteen months, between 1959 and 1960, the ship's company consumed a total of 152 oxen, which had to be prepared for the galley staff by the two specially trained Royal Marine butchers in the beef screen.

Left: Every day, the six bakers used these electric ovens to produce at least fifty-two 4lb loaves and 1,440 bread rolls, in addition to the 200lb of pies, pastries, cakes and buns that were made per week to satisfy the healthy appetites of over seven hundred men. A further 8,740lb of bread was also baked each week to cater for the men onboard the smaller ships that operated in company with *Belfast* and had no means of producing their own bread.

Above: Every department nominated one rating each day to assist the galley staff in the vegetable preparation room, where peeling and chipping machines transformed the execution of an otherwise monotonous yet essential daily chore. The size of the task is illustrated by the fact that the ship's company ate 536,350lb of potatoes between May 1959 and August 1960.

Bottom left: To keep up with the huge demand for bread in *Belfast*, everything had to be done on a large scale, from the kneader for the dough, which looked more like a concrete mixer, to the storage shelves for the baked bread.

Bottom right: *Belfast*'s storerooms acted as a magnet for any rats which had managed to find their way on board the ship. To counter the threat posed by rodents, most warships carried at least one cat until 1975, when for hygiene reasons the Admiralty banned all animals from HM ships.

Top left: The implementation of Cafeteria Messing during *Belfast*'s 1956–59 modernisation resulted in a significant improvement in the living conditions of the ratings. Instead of eating in their individual messes, the leading rates and below helped themselves from the choice dishes available along the serving counter, situated along the port side of the galley. Having placed their food in a recessed self-service tray, they carried it across to the nearby common canteen, known as the ship's company dining hall, where they sat down to eat the meal. This change enabled the professionally trained cooks to offer a wider selection of food that could be served hotter and fresher than had previously been possible. The meals were prepared in bulk by the twenty-six cooks who worked in four watches to prepare some 18,000 meals per week. Their facilities included ovens, boiling coppers (bottom), roasters, grills and fryers.

Middle left: Even though the galley was relatively spacious, it could be a difficult environment in which to work, especially in the Far East where temperatures of well over 100°F (38°C) were not uncommon. To illustrate the amount of food consumed by the ship's company on a weekly basis, the records show that a total of 5,600 sausages, 3,500 eggs, 56cwt of potatoes, and 180 boxes of cereal were eaten every week for breakfast in 1959. Separate galleys were located elsewhere in the ship to prepare meals for the admiral, captain, officers and senior rates.

Opposite, top: A general view of the relatively spacious galley. In addition to their normal catering duties, fourteen of the cooks served as a gun crew for one of the 4in mountings between 1959 and 1961.

Opposite, bottom: The former ship's company dining hall is now reserved for the private functions organised by Sodexo Prestige which make an important financial contribution towards *Belfast*'s preservation. *(Courtesy Sodexo Prestige)*

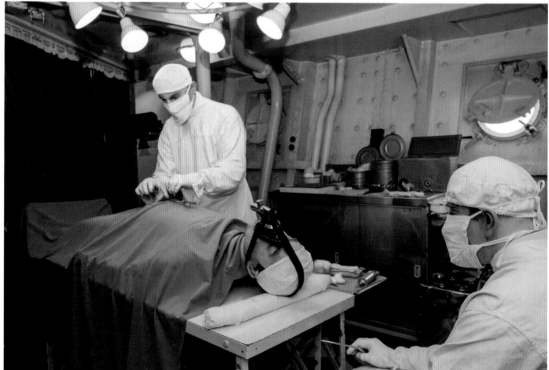

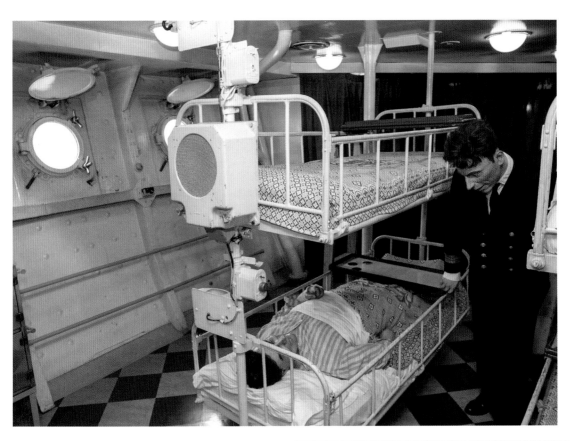

Opposite, top: Primarily responsible for looking after the dental health of the ship's company, the dental officer, usually a surgeon lieutenant commander, was also an important member of the ship's medical team. Due to the precision required for this kind of work, he carried out the majority of his routine appointments whenever *Belfast* was in harbour to avoid the complications caused by the ship's motion at sea.

Opposite: For peacetime deployments, *Belfast* usually carried a medical staff of seven which consisted of two surgeons and five supporting sick berth attendants including a radiographer and physiotherapist. The sick bay facilities included an operating theatre, four pivoting cots, bathrooms, a consulting room, dispensary and the neighbouring dental surgery.

The medical staff's routine work included examinations, minor treatments, and vaccinations. It also dealt with any medical emergencies onboard *Belfast* and smaller ships in the vicinity as well as occasionally providing assistance to remote coastal communities that did not have access to hospital services. During the Korean War, *Belfast's* medical team operated on thirty casualties brought onboard as a result of incidents onshore and five emergency abdominal operations. In the same period, the sick bay dispensed a total of 18,000 aspirins, 11,000 codeine tablets, 49,500 sulpha tablets, 1,373,000,000 units of penicillin and used 35½ miles of bandages as well as 594lbs of cotton wool and lint.

Above: The sick bay's ward contained four cots for patients to recuperate in. Although the cots were pivoted, to counter the rolling of *Belfast* from side to side, nothing could be done about the pitching of the ship.

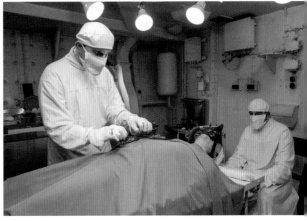

Bottom right: The surgeons only carried out major operations within the sick bay in an emergency due to the increased risk posed by the movement and vibration of the ship. However, when required, the operating theatre could be closed off by curtains and was sufficiently equipped to cater for most routine operations. For example, during *Belfast's* final transatlantic crossing, the principal medical officer successfully operated on a member of the ship's company who developed acute appendicitis. In a fortunate twist of fate, the HMS *Belfast* Trust managed to secure the original surgical instruments that were used onboard the ship during her final years in commission.

Above and left: This chief petty officer's messdeck illustrates the significant step change in the ratings' living conditions that was achieved by the conversion from Broadside Messing to Canteen Messing during *Belfast*'s 1956–59 modernisation. The traditional hammocks gave way to bunks mounted in three tiers and equipped with Dunlopillo mattresses. Although the ratings no longer ate in the mess, the space occupied by the bunks was also used for recreation. To achieve this, the middle bunk could be folded back to transform the two lower bunks in to a settee for use when the sailors were off duty. Folding tables were brought out to provide a suitable surface for games, ash trays, drinks, etc. The kit lockers on the right-hand side of the image contained each person's belongings while the space above was used to store their suit cases. Despite the changes, space remained at a premium. For example, the end of each row of kit lockers provided the perfect place to mount a mirror, coat hooks, and wash basin. The amount of cutlery and crockery issued to the individual messdecks was also reduced following the change to Canteen Messing to simply provide enough for making tea and coffee as well as receiving the tot of rum.

Opposite, above: The port side triple torpedo tubes were originally mounted in this section of 02 deck before *Belfast*'s modernisation when they were removed and the open firing ports were plated over. Some of this freed up space was then reused to provide new offices for the Drafting and Leave sections.

Opposite, below: Even though *Belfast* did not rely on any form of sail power, her resident sailmaker was kept fully employed by making and repairing a long list of items including awnings, boat covers and gun covers.

Top left: During *Belfast*'s time in commission, every rating over the age of twenty was entitled to receive one tot (one eighth of a pint) of rum each day or to be given a cash allowance. This cherished naval tradition dated back to 1687 when the Royal Navy introduced a daily issue of rum in place of brandy. Men were entitled to one pint of neat rum per day, while boys were given half a pint. In 1740, Admiral Edward Vernon, universally known as 'Old Grog' due to the grogram boat cloak he always wore, tried to reduce the amount of drunkenness caused by this policy in the Fleet by giving orders to water down the ration with two parts water to one part rum and splitting the daily issue into two halves. The first half was to be administered at noon followed by the other half at 1800. He also stated that the rum should be

distributed to the tune of 'Nancy Dawson' from a cut-down cask, known as a 'grog-tub' or 'scuttle-butt', which was traditionally embellished with the words 'The King [or Queen] God Bless Him [or Her]' in brass letters. The watered-down drink swiftly became known as 'grog'. Subsequent orders reduced the amount of rum that was issued as well as the number of qualifying personnel. However, the Royal Navy's sailors regarded it as one of their most important privileges until its abolition on 31 July 1970. The dilution of the rum for leading rates and below always took place in the presence of an officer to protect the sailors' interests and any surplus rum had to be poured into the scuppers to prevent its misuse. Chief petty officers and petty officers were issued with neat rum.

Below left: The open hatch on the left-hand side of this image leads down to the shell room for 'B' turret. The provision issue room can be seen through the open half-door whilst the wooden frame that can be seen towards the right-hand side of the image is one of the two counters for the Navy Army and Air Force Institute's (NAAFI) Canteen. The ship's company could buy a wide selection of items from this shop including duty-free tobacco, toothpaste, writing paper, and shoe polish. A percentage of the profits that were made by the NAAFI were ploughed back into the canteen fund which was managed by a committee and could be spent on items to improve the welfare of the ship's company as a whole.

Above: The captain could imprison sailors for up to fourteen days for offences such as leave-breaking, sleeping on watch or drunkenness. The cell's position, right up in the bows, added to the severity of being confined to the austere, claustrophobic environment of the cell, if the sentence coincided with a spell of rough weather, due to the increased rise and fall that would have been experienced at hull's extremities. The cell's 'amenities' consisted of a hard wooden pillow, a bare unpadded bunk and a copy of the Bible. Apart from reading the Bible, the only other activity on offer to the offending sailor was 'picking oakum' which consisted of unravelling hard rope that had been impregnated with tar.

THE ARCTIC MESSDECK

THE FORWARD MESSDECKS HAVE BEEN returned to how they would have appeared during the era of Broadside Messing to illustrate the living conditions that were experienced by *Belfast's* sailors for the majority of her time in commission. 120 ratings lived, ate and slept in the three messdecks that form this exhibit. Living in such a confined environment could be tough. To prosper in these circumstances, ratings relied on a mixture of friendliness, cheerfulness, discipline and a good sense of humour. To help pass the time whilst off duty, the sailors frequently organised competitions in their messdecks for various card and board games including 'uckers' (Ludo), crib, draughts and chess.

All of the food was cooked centrally in the ship's galley. To cope with the less than ideal method of distribution, it was generally stodgy and unimaginative, although rarely in short supply. The senior hand of the mess organised a daily roster to nominate one rating to act as cook of the mess. The chosen sailor prepared the food in the messdeck and took it to the galley to be cooked. When it was ready, he collected the meals from the galley and served out the food. Afterwards, he would clean up and return all of the dishes and utensils that had been borrowed from the galley. The remaining cutlery and crockery was kept in lockers in the messdeck. Some of the cook's other duties included collecting the rum issue, unless the messdeck had a designated 'rum bosun', making the stand-easy tea, and replenishing the messdeck's supply of tea, sugar and milk from the stores.

Main image: Despite the IWM's current policy of removing barriers whenever possible, they have been retained in the Arctic Messdeck to deter souvenir hunters from acquiring the various small personal items that are on display to illustrate the daily lives of the sailors in their messdecks.

Bottom right: The lockers against the ship's side contained the messdeck's cutlery, crockery and refreshments. A hinged solid metal plate, known as the deadlight, can be seen next to the locker. It can be secured across the scuttle and was used to either preserve the scuttle's watertight integrity in the event of the glass being broken, or to assist the darkening of the ship when required. In hot climates, windscoops were fitted to the outside of the scuttles to assist the air circulation throughout the living spaces.

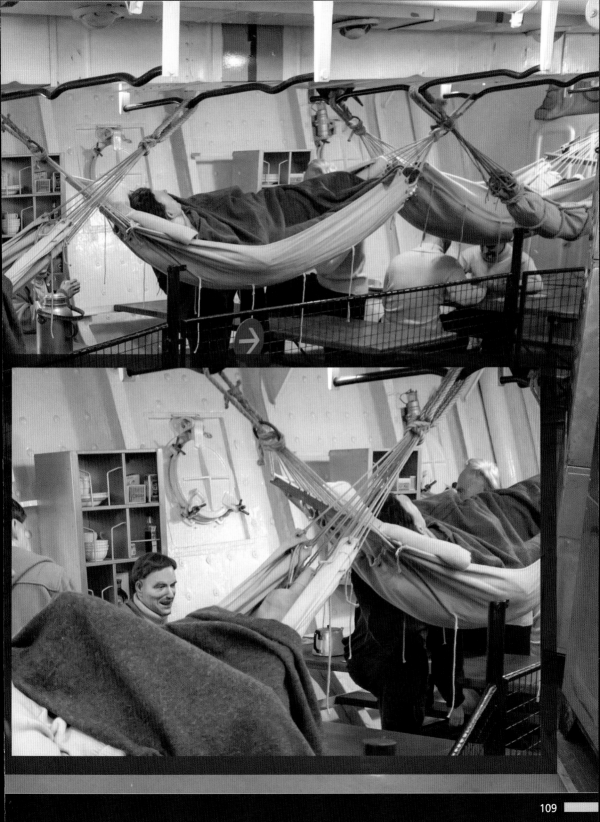

Left: Sailors had to be accommodated wherever space could be found, including either side of the 6in turret supports, which resulted in some extremely cramped living conditions. The problem became particularly serious during WWII with the need to accommodate the additional sailors needed to operate the often bulky new items of equipment.

Above: Sailors slung their hammocks just 21in apart, from the overhead metal bars that were attached to the deckhead. In the morning they were required to lash up their hammocks and either trice them up to the beams or nettings. When circumstances permitted, they would be aired up on deck.

Middle right: Letters provided the only form of contact between the sailors and their families.

Bottom right: In 1943, one of *Belfast*'s cats, Frankenstein, was trained to sleep in his own miniature hammock. In addition to their rat catching duties, the ship's cats were identified by a conference of naval chaplains at the beginning of WWII as an effective means of boosting morale. It had been observed on several occasions before the war that the presence of a pet onboard a ship managed to transform the behaviour of troublesome sailors by providing a welcome distraction from their grievances. The more endearing ship's cats were often adopted as official mascots either by the ship as a whole or by individual messdecks. Whilst the majority of animals carried by the Royal Navy's warships were either cats or dogs, more exotic creatures were sometimes embarked, such as orang-utans, parrots, geese, and in *Belfast*'s case, briefly a young female antelope called Olga, presented by the Russian Admiral Golovko in December 1943.

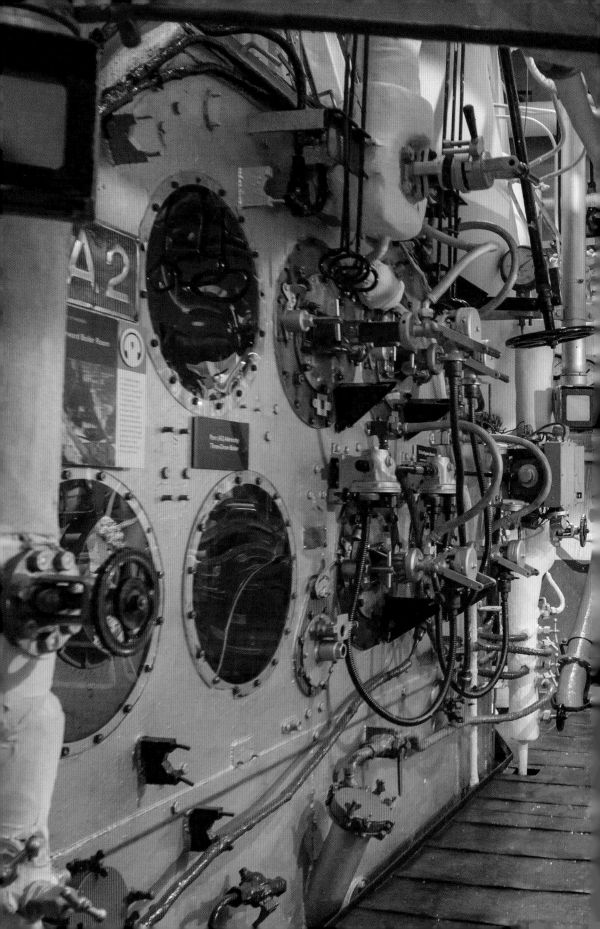

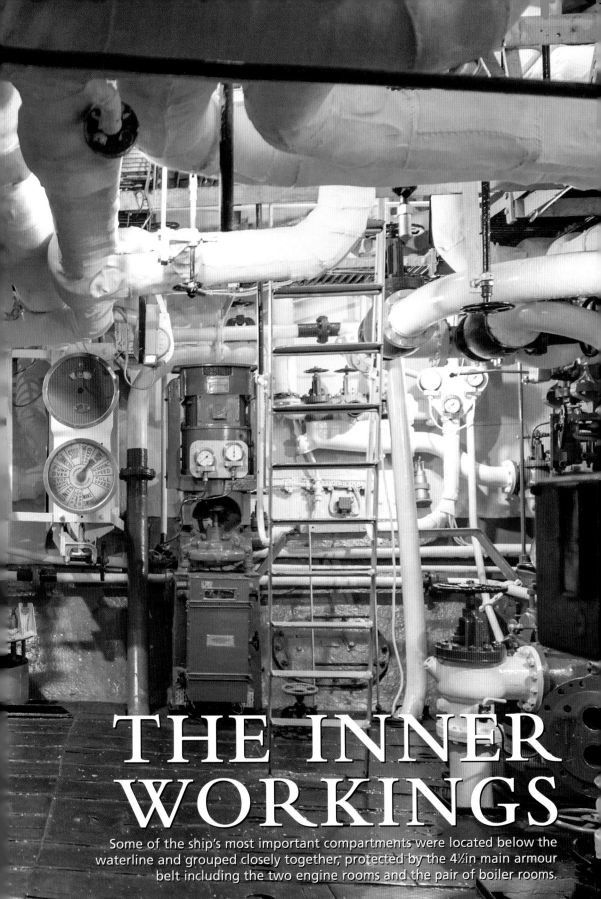

THE INNER
WORKINGS

Some of the ship's most important compartments were located below the
waterline and grouped closely together, protected by the 4½in main armour
belt including the two engine rooms and the pair of boiler rooms.

Left and below: Packed full of equipment including the gunnery radar displays and the starshell calculator, the bulk of the 6in transmitting station is taken up with a mechanical calculating machine, the Admiralty fire control table (AFCT) Mark VI, which converted the information provided by the forward director control tower into the elevation and training required by the 6in guns.

Opposite, bottom left: A close-up view of the deflection dial and three line of sight dials on the top of the AFCT.

Opposite, bottom right: A close-up of the two director setting dials on the top of the AFCT.

Bottom left: The Dumaresq Wheel: mechanical analogue fire control instrument used to calculate the relative motion between two ships to determine range and deflection.

Bottom middle: The bombardment spotting disc and bombardment line spotting conversion disc.

Bottom right: A smaller version of the AFCT, known as the Admiralty fire control clock, was located in the neighbouring compartment and provided the same type of information for 'X' and 'Y' turrets only.

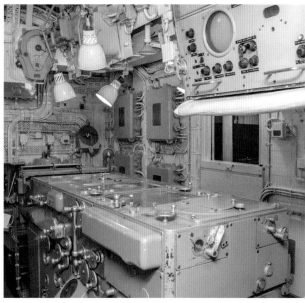

Above left: Moving the traditional wooden ship's wheel operated transmitter rams which pumped hydraulic fluid, consisting of glycerine and distilled water, to and from the receiver rams in the tiller flat. To reduce the chances of a complete failure due to battle damage, the hydraulic system is fitted in duplicate. The brass lever at the top of the pedestal indicates the wheel's position while the two brass dials underneath enabled the helmsman to monitor the pressure in each side of the hydraulic system.

To increase redundancy, many of the systems in the forward steering position were fitted in duplicate or even triplicate including the rudder position indicators and the dials used to display the ship's speed.

Opposite, top: The ship's telephone exchange is located in the compartment beside the forward steering position.

Above right: The forward steering position acted as the primary steering point for the ship and the place from which the engine orders were transmitted to the appropriate engine rooms, using the combined engine order and revolution telegraphs mounted either side of the traditional wooden ship's wheel. Situated six decks below the compass platform, the helmsman and the two telegraph men received their orders via the conning broadcast.

Right: The port side combined engine order and revolution telegraph. Alterations to either the engine revolutions or direction could be transmitted to the engine room by turning the appropriate handle on the side of the telegraph. The numerals and brass lever on top of the telegraph displayed the latest settings ordered by the officer of the watch on the compass platform.

Middle left: The four reply gongs, mounted on the bulkhead between the two compartments, were used by the appropriate engine room to acknowledge a change in engine order. Each gong was differently toned and reserved for one of the four shafts. The standard code for this purpose was: slow, one ring; half, two rings; full, three rings; and stop, two double rings.

Middle right: The navigation compass worked on the gyroscopic principle, ensuring that it always pointed true north regardless of the ship's movements. In addition to enabling the ship to be accurately helmed, it provided the information to co-ordinate the radars and fire control systems. To reduce the threat posed by equipment failure, *Belfast* was fitted with gyro-compasses in two separate compartments. The active gyro-compass was connected to the repeaters on the compass platform, forward steering position and the admiral's bridge.

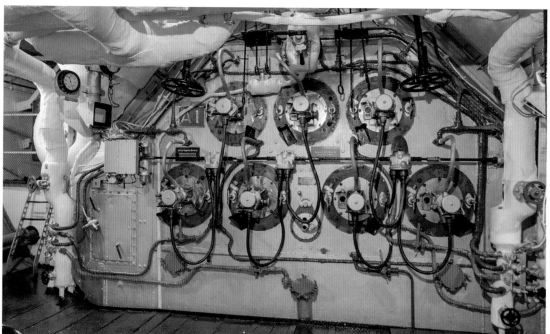

Above: The engine order telegraph by A2 boiler.

Below: The interior of a water drum. The rows of holes are the lower ends of the generator tubes which connect the water drum to the steam drum.

IN 1931 IT WAS DECIDED TO ADOPT THE UNIT system of machinery in the design of the cruiser HMS *Amphion* (later HMAS *Perth*). Previously, all the boilers were situated within a single compartment and all of the engines were located in another. The new layout, which was adopted in every subsequent British cruiser including *Belfast*, lowered the risk of a single hit causing a total loss of power by splitting the machinery between four compartments alternating boiler room, engine room, boiler room, engine room. Cross connections enabled each boiler room to supply either engine room. However, this scheme increased the length required for the machinery spaces, the amount of armour needed, and the number of personnel.

Above left: The forward boiler room. On the right-hand side can be seen the oil fuel pumps which brought a heavy oil mixture known as furnace fuel oil (FFO) to the two Admiralty-type three-drum water tube boilers within this compartment.

Bottom left: The Admiralty-type three-drum water tube boiler A1 in the forward boiler room. Each boiler consists of two equal-sized water drums connected by rows of steel tubes, known as generator tubes, to a larger steam drum above them to form an inverted 'V' shape above the furnace, lined with fire bricks. Seven oil fuel burners on the front of the boiler supplied the FFO under pressure to the furnace where it was burnt. As the oil burned, the combustion gases passed upwards and boiled the water circulating in the generator tubes to create super-heated steam at a pressure of 350lb/sq in. This collected in the upper steam drum and was piped to the turbines in the engine room to drive the propeller shafts.

Above: *Belfast's* forward engine room. The pair of engines in this compartment drove the two outer propeller shafts while the engines in the aft engine room drove the two inner shafts. Each engine was capable of delivering 20,000shp to create a total output of 80,000shp which drove the ship to a maximum speed of 32 knots. To achieve the desired speed, each engine was connected to four turbine rotors consisting of a high and low pressure turbine which could be used together to achieve full power ahead; a smaller cruising turbine to deliver more economical speeds; and an astern turbine.

Left: The bell on top of this combined engine order and revolution telegraph would ring to signal a change in either engine orders or revolution by the officer of the watch up on the compass platform.

Opposite, top: Each of these wheels opened and closed the valves which controlled the flow of super-heated steam to the chosen combination of turbine rotors that were connected to the port outer engine.

Opposite, middle left: Looking down the vertical steel ladder that leads to the deck on which the port outer engine's gear box is mounted.

Opposite, middle right: The high pressure turbine is one of four turbines that are connected to the starboard outer engine. Its cover has been lifted to reveal the blades.

Opposite, bottom left: This counter displays the total number of revolutions for the starboard outer propeller shaft.

Opposite, bottom right: The port outer engine.

CONSERVATION

Belfast's ongoing maintenance is undertaken by a mixture of employed members of staff and a growing band of volunteers. Each of the latter is assigned to a specific team working on a long-term restoration project such as the renovation of the aft starboard 40mm Bofors, enabling the employed conservation staff to tackle more urgent tasks.

FUTURE RESTORATION PROJECTS INCLUDE THE close-range blind fire director (above left) and 40mm Bofors gun mounting (above right) on the starboard side of the aft superstructure.

The way in which ongoing renovation work is carried out has changed since 1971. Then the key objective was to ensure the public's safety, replacing items before they posed a threat to either the visitors or the ship's future. Whilst this remains of paramount importance, the workers also try to conserve the ship's original fabric whenever possible. This subtle change in approach is reflected in her status as a historical artefact in the IWM's collection with the catalogue number MAR 555.

Another significant change in recent years is the increasing importance of the growing band of Warship Conservation Volunteers in the fulfilment of the ship's conservation plan. Although a few unpaid individuals had been involved in *Belfast*'s preservation since she opened to the public, the active recruitment and development of a specific volunteer group did not occur until September 2006 when the IWM created the post of volunteer co-ordinator for its London branches. At the time of writing, *Belfast*'s group consists of thirty-nine people who are aged between eighteen and eighty-five. They have a wide range of backgrounds, experience and skill sets. Some have previous engi-

neering or metalworking experience while others are just history enthusiasts keen to do something practical in a heritage environment. Even though the majority are London-based, a few regularly travel from as far as Nottinghamshire, Coventry and Wiltshire. The scale of their input is underlined by the group's contribution of 2,413 days or 14,478 hours of labour towards *Belfast*'s preservation between October 2006 and March 2011. Most of their work involves the renovation of machinery, the ship's armament and other equipment exposed to the elements on the upper decks, although they have also restored enclosed areas such as the admiral's bridge.

Top: Maintaining *Belfast* requires a careful juggling act between taking advantage of favourable weather windows to carry out external work, and ensuring that visitors do not feel that they are in the middle of a building site. The Conservation Manager always schedules the noisiest jobs, such as stripping down metalwork for repainting, while the ship is closed, which can lead to some very early mornings and late nights for the conservation team.

Above: The Hotchkiss 3pdr saluting gun situated on the port side of the aft superstructure is another future restoration project for the volunteers. Four were originally fitted during *Belfast*'s construction and removed in 1942.

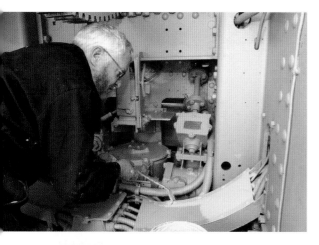

Left: A volunteer carries out the finishing touches to the two and a half year long restoration of the forward 4in mounting on the starboard side.

Middle, left: Whilst the opening up of items such as this steam-driven fire and bilge pump may seem at odds with the IWM's conservation policy, it turns an otherwise uninspiring piece of equipment into an intriguing exhibit which is more likely to capture the attention of the ship's visitors.

Opposite, top: The admiral's sea cabin on 02 deck of the forward superstructure is another area that is due to be assigned to a team of volunteers as a long-term restoration project.

Below: Smaller items of equipment are usually removed and brought to the small workshop located by the forward funnel where they can be refurbished behind closed doors. Since 1971 the conservation team have tried to recover or replace the various items of equipment that were removed after she paid off into reserve in 1963. In 1974 the Royal Navy contributed towards the restoration of her external profile by donating four 40mm Bofors mountings along with six close-range blind fire directors to replace the missing originals. During the 1970s and 1980s the conservation team established good relations with the various HM naval bases to gain access to decommissioned ships that had been fitted with the same type of equipment as *Belfast*. These opportunities have led to several important acquisitions ranging in size from large items of equipment to smaller fittings such as lampshades and switch panels. Scrap yards have also proved to be a useful source of spares although timing is always of the essence in such situations. Inevitably, these sources are beginning to run dry as the final surviving warships to have served in the Royal Navy during the 1960s and 1970s are broken up for scrap.

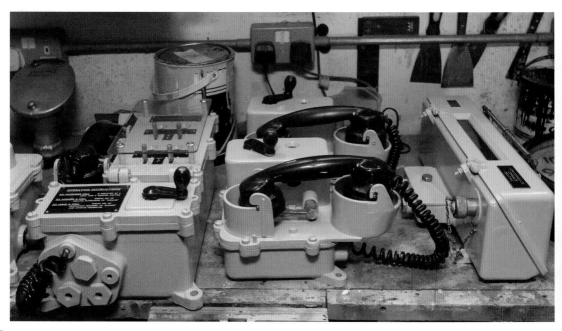

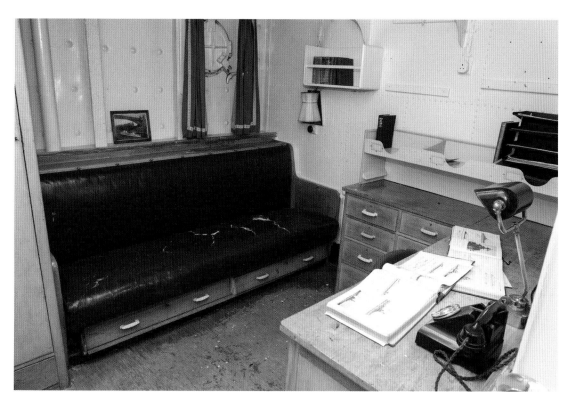

Right: Props like these can still make a difference when presenting areas, such as the admiral's sea cabin, that have yet to benefit from a full-scale restoration. The presentation of several compartments throughout the ship has been enriched by the steady trickle of personal effects that have been donated over the years by those who served in *Belfast*. The value of these items can not be underestimated because they help the IWM to create a more realistic impression of life on board.

Bottom left: A gyro tape repeater and clock in the process of being refurbished on a workbench within the discreet workshop by the forward funnel.

Bottom right: The conservation team has now completed its renovation of these switches and telephones which can be returned to their original positions.

BIBLIOGRAPHY

BR 1938 Naval Ratings Handbook (Ministry of Defence Naval Training Department, London, 1965)

BR 3003 ('I) Naval Marine Engineering Practice Volume I (Her Majesty's Stationery Office, London, 1959)

Brown, David, *Tirpitz: The Floating Fortress* (Arms And Armour Press, London, 1977)

Brown, David K, *Warrior To Dreadnought: Warship Development 1860–1905* (Chatham Publishing, London, 1997)

Brown, David K, *Nelson To Vanguard, Warship Development 1923–1945* (Seaforth Publishing, Barnsley, 2012)

Burns, K V, Lt Cdr, *Badges And Battle Honours of HM Ships* (Maritime Books, Liskeard, 1986)

Busch, Fritz-Otto, Corvette Captain, *The Drama of the Scharnhorst* (Robert Hale Ltd, London, 1956)

Campbell, John, *Naval Weapons of World War II* (Conway Maritime Press, London, 1985)

Churchill, Winston, *The Second World War* (Cassell, London, Volume I 1948, Volume II 1949, Volume III 1950, Volume IV 1951, Volume V 1952 & Volume VI 1954)

Curran, Andy, *HMS Belfast Conservation Policy 2012* (Imperial War Museum, London, 2012)

Earl, Lawrence, *The Story of HMS Amethyst* (George G Harrap & Co, London, 1950)

Edwards, Commander Kenneth, *Operation Neptune* (Collins, London, 1946)

Evans, David, *Arming the Fleet* (Explosion! Museum of Naval Firepower, Gosport, in association with English Heritage, 2006)

Farrar-Hockley, Anthony, *The British Part in the Korean War* (Her Majesty's Stationery Office, London, Volume 1 1990, Volume 2 1995)

Field, James A, *History of United States Naval Operations Korea* (US Government Printing Office, Washington, 1962)

Finch, George E, *Tiffy: The Autobiography of a Naval Engineer* (Square One Publications, Worcester, 1991)

Fox, Uffa, *Sail and Power* (Peter Davies Ltd, London 1936)

Friedman, Norman, *British Cruisers: Two World Wars and After* (Seaforth Publishing, Barnsley, 2010)

Grove, Eric, *Vanguard to Trident* (Naval Institute Press, Annapolis, 1987)

Hart-Davis, Duff, *King's Counsellor Abdication and War: The Diaries of Sir Alan Lascelles* (Weidenfeld & Nicholson, London, 2006)

HMS Belfast 1950–1952 The Record of a Commission (Imperial War Museum, London, 2005)

HMS Belfast 1961–1962 (Imperial War Museum, London, 2005)

Hobbs, David, *The British Pacific Fleet: The Royal Navy's Most Powerful Strike Force* (Seaforth Publishing, Barnsley, 2011)

Howarth, Stephen, *The Royal Navy's Reserves in War & Peace 1903–2003* (Leo Cooper, Barnsley, 2003)

Humble, Richard, *Fraser of North Cape* (Routledge & Kegan Paul, London, 1983)

Imperial War Museum, *HMS Belfast* (Imperial War Museum, London, 1999)

Imperial War Museum, *HMS Belfast* (Imperial War Museum, London, 2009)

Manual of Seamanship Volume 1 (His Majesty's Stationery Office, London, 1932)

Manual of Seamanship Volume 1 (His Majesty's Stationery Office, London, 1951)

Manual of Seamanship Volume 1 (Her Majesty's Stationery Office, London, 1964)

Kemp, Peter, *The Oxford Companion to Ships and the Sea* (Granada Publishing Ltd, London 1979)

Lewis, Val, *Ships' Cats in War and Peace* (Nauticalia Ltd, Shepperton-on-Thames, 2001)

Morgan-Giles, Rear Admiral Sir Morgan, *The Unforgiving Minute* (Clarendon Press,' Wotton-under-Edge, 2002)

Moss, Michael, & Hume, John R, *Shipbuilders to the World: 125 Years of Harland and Wolff, Belfast 1861–1986* (The Blackstaff Press, Belfast, 1986)

Ogden, Michael, Lt Cdr, *The Battle of North Cape* (William Kimber & Co, London, 1962)

Preston, Anthony, *Cruisers: An Illustrated History 1880–1980* (Arms & Armour Press, London, 1980)

Roskill, Stephen, *The War At Sea* (Her Majesty's Stationery Office, London, Volume I 1954, Volume II 1956, Volume III Part I 1960 & Volume III Part II 1961)

Roskill, Stephen, *Naval Policy Between The Wars, Volume 2 The Period Of Reluctant Rearmament 1930–1939* (Collins, London, 1976)

Schofield, Brian Betham, Vice Admiral, *Operation Neptune* (Ian Allen, Shepperton, 1974)

Simkins, Peter, *HMS Belfast* (Imperial War Museum, London, 1982)

Smith, Ernest E, *Men of the Sea* (Melrose Books, Ely, 2006)

Smith, Oliver M, *HMS Belfast* (The Macmillan Press Ltd, 1971)

Townsend, John, Instr Lt Cdr, *HMS Belfast Far East Station 1959–61* (Ye Olde Printerie Ltd, Hong Kong, 1961)